Biafra rising in woto-woto and **rantings of an angry Man by Iwunna Uwanuruochi.**

This work is dedicated to the estimated 3 million Biafran children starved to death, to Biafrans and foreign supporters killed during the immediate circumstances of the genocide of the world against Biafra from 1966 to 1970 and to many more, to about one million Biafrans that have been killed from 1970 to 2024. To Mazi Nnamdi Kanu languishing in prison for demanding self-determination for his people. to Mazi Simon Ekpa PM his cabinet, BRGIE, the men of BLA, BRF, BAF, BMF all MOG and to the entire Biafran people.

Synopsis

Biafra lost its independence through British colonial conquests in the late 17th century. Throughout the years of colonialism, Biafra never accepted subjugation at the hands of Britain. In 1914, the British governor general amalgamated the hitherto independent indigenous communities of Biafra with the Northern nations. The reason given was for ease of governance, as the southern states are very rich in natural resources, the northern region would benefit if the two regions were merged into one. Amalgamation was not able to unify the peoples of these different nations due to their natural differences in every aspect of their existence. Being forced together had had the singular result of unending conflicts throughout the last 300 years. A war had been fought and consistent genocide is the resut of the unending conflict in the country known as Nigeria. The eastern region have again risen to extricate itself from the carnage life have turned out to be for the peoples. This time around, they have challenged violence with resistance first by peaceful demonstration; this was met with armed violence against the indigenous people by Nigeria. Indigenous people responded by declaring sit-at-home once a year. Nigeria started indiscriminate killings. In 2016, more than 100 youths gathered for prayers at Aba were killed there at the field. Nigeria declared operation python dance at which the army tried to kill the leader of the Biafran movement. He escaped, but 28 people were killed and the parents of the leader died in the aftermath of the assault. Today, woto-woto is the message from the army and woto-woto is the response because Biafra have refused to back down.

Contents

The Biafran question

In the beginning, they say, is the best place to start telling any story. Our story started in the beginning, when we inherited from ChukwuOkikeAbiama, the lands of the rising sun. A pristine holy territory of brave and courageous men, a land of beautiful maidens, a land where the songs of its forests and waters tell its stories in our hearts. Biafra is the holiest of all the lands on earth. I am claiming this right, because it has become apparent that every other race and ethnicities on earth will stop at nothing to disposes us of our land, the lands of Biafra. It was the Spanish and the Portuguese, then the British, the Germans, now these same nations are using proxy nations of Fulani, Hausa and other Nigerian ethnicities to prevent the emancipation of Biafra. How had it come to this, that in the 21st century, there is a people still fighting for independence for over 600 years. Why have they not been conquered? Why are they still fighting and who are their enemies?

This document does not attempt to trace the genesis of Biafra, their disposition to life or the characteristics of their indigenous peoples. It explores the question 'why 1966-1970 war had not ended for the supposed winners of that genocidal onslaught 50 years after the fact and counting?

During the days of that ignominious war, we fought with every heartbeat we could muster. They came against us, the greatest military powers of those days and their minions with everything they had. It felt like the insistent pattering of thunderstorm mid rainy season, on the thatched roof of our houses at night. Beating down relentlessly drowning every tear and soaking the bravest of heart in its wake. What had the palm tree done but produce leaves? What is the man's sin? He harvested the leaves and produced thatch for to roof a round earthen structure wherein he and his wife may live and raise a family. A home is their intent, to raise a few children and pass on to them the knowledge and skills

of living in the heartland of the east. So why is the rain angry? Why couldn't thunder and lightning take their battles out to sea, where no one but the poor fishes may complain.
They came down on us raining brimstone and fires on schools, and churches and market places. There was no water to assuage the thirst we felt, they knew, they used it to coin a name for us 'nyamiri' ("Nyem mmiri" the cry of every captured soldier asking for water to assuage thirst). Yet the storm continued unabated, Amaamilo once asked Papa, "was it something we did at the farms, the lands we tilled and prepared to harvest the rains, for now, the clouds send a storm not rain?"
"Why do you think so?" Papa had countered.
"Because it appears the storm is attempting to tear down our house Papa!"
"Ha ha ha! we only respond when the heavens speak to us, but we cannot give up, tomorrow we repair our homes and attend to the farms. This is the homeland, it is nature as it had always been."
Just as the rain breaks after a storm, we rose again in 1970. It was very deadly, many lives and properties were lost. We survived, when estimated 3 million died. Amaamilo and Iwunna ate lizards and grasshoppers thanks to their cousin. She was just a couple of years older than their 2 and 1 years of age. She was our minder in those days, Papa was in the war effort. We only saw our mother sometimes at night. Mma was very young and beautiful, so she had to hide or the invading soldiers would take her away from the homeland.
That was in the beginning if you ask me. My great grandfather slapped a young apprentice of his, who happen to be his cousin, this happened sometime between 1820 to 1830. In the succeeding years, some of Okorie's children moved from Amakama to their present home today, Amaimo. In 1925 a man allegedly said to me: 'I have not forgotten your great grandfather's assault on my great grandfather while teaching his own cousin how to make baskets at

Amakama in the 1800s'. It was a wake-up call for me, you could never get me within ten yards of Nwamara till this day. That is its tale and its own story.

I watched the pogrom documents, graphic and disturbing as they were, papa did not remove them from our house library. I thank ChukwuOkikeAbiama that he did, because we may not have realized in time what dangers we face or the character of our enemies. While we moved on, they remained stuck to the war years, yearning and missing the time when they could kill, maim and ravage as they wish and be lauded for it. They apparently missed the destruction, burning of homes and farm fields, desecration of every holy of holies. They missed the days of having brave Biafran men kneel to beg them for their very lives after being ambushed, caught in the tickets and trapped like a beast. They missed their bravado earned with rounds upon rounds of Egyptian fighter jets strafing Biafran homes and markets to soften targets before they would flow in like flood debris to pillage and ravage the homes of dead men and women littering the village squares or hanging on trees where they sought refuge. That maybe one reason they had not moved on.

Papa returned home to show Mma the 20 pounds he received from the bank in lieu of every monies they both had saved through 8 years as senior government servants. Sadly, they had closed both their bank accounts and opened a joint account after their marriage in 1966 or Mma would had also received another 20 pounds but that was not to be. 20 pounds for a family of 4. Mma was pregnant by this time too.

Papa did not want to immortalize or give any special attention to that very 20 pounds. Mma could not remember what it was used for, they called it blood money and so lost it to the homeland somehow as they moved. They returned to work and by the next month, their lives were back on course. Our tears we left where we found them hoping never to go back to them; however, life has surprises for us in time.

Tightening Some Screws

“What do you mean by problem candidate?” I asked Papa

“I do not really know, this is a new issue but I will check tomorrow”

Papa returned from school the next day to tell us that we will sit exams as everyone else, the ‘problem’ happened at the exam board not the individual schools. But the damage was already done. My senior brother and I aced the exams as the best candidates from our school. At every exams following my Common entrance, I will eagerly wait, check and crosscheck my documents a million times. I was never sure of myself until I receive my results months later; just because once at 10 years of age, after I registered exams, the exams board reported they could not find my name on the school list, making me and others sit exams as “problem candidate.”

The definition of indigenous persons or people should be looked into. We cannot keep moving blindly because there is a need to understand what we are up against, which would sharpen our quest or redirect our method of agitation against subjugation in the Nigerian enterprise.

As a people that have ability, we need to be calculative and precise. I am once again stressing the need for the use of our learned personalities in this quest for self-determination. We should understand the reluctance of these class of persons among us to commit to using their knowledge and time to fight our course as a nation.

Today I am using the United Nations articles and documents freely available in the public domain to place Biafra squarely in the category of Nations that fully deserve international attention and a nation that need this urgently like say: YESTERDAY!

The fact sheet of the United Nations permanent forum on indigenous issues defines indigenous people as “people who practice a unique tradition, retaining social, cultural, economic and political characteristics distinct from another dominant society among them". They must be "descendants of those who inhabited a country or geographical area before the arrival of the different ethnicities which are now dominant over them, through conquest, occupation, settlement or other means."

All the different ethnicities of eastern Nigeria qualify under the above definition as indigenous peoples of Biafra.

Anang, Abua, Abayon, Agbo, Akaju-Ndem, Andoni, Anioma, Anyima, Bachere, Bahumono, Bekwarra, Bette, Bille, Bini, Boki, Ebira, Ebu, Efik, Egbema, Egede, Ejegham, Ekajuk, Eket, Ekoi, Ekpeye, Epie, Esan, Ekid, Etche, Etsako, Etung, Etuno, Gokana, Ibani, Ibeno, Ibibio, Ibo, Idoma, Igala, Ijaw, Ika, Ikom, Ikwerre, Iman, Isoko, Itsekiri, Itu, ItuMbioUso, Iyala, Joinkrama, Kalabari, Kugbo, Mbembe, Mbube, Ngene, Nkim, Nkum, Obolo, Ododop, Ogoni, Ogori, Ogba. Okobo, Okirika, Okpamheri, Olukumi, Oron, Ososo, Owan, Qua, Udekeama, Ufia, Ukelle, Kwale, Ineme, Urhobo, Utonkong, Uwanno, Uyanga, Yache, Yako.

(I may have left out some or included non-Biafran ethnicities above. I do not claim to be an expert on this identification process and so I crave your indulgence and demand that those ethnicities so left out be included by you and please point out those that are not Biafran ethnicities too).

All these ethnicities of South Eastern Nigeria have retained their identities from time immemorial. They can all trace their ancestry to hundreds of thousands of years before colonialism, why then the imposition of the Nigerian Nation on all of them. We need to delve into the intricate issues of the requirement:

"have retained distinct characteristics which are clearly different from those of other segments of the national population"

We point to the clear demarcation of ethnicities in Nigeria as a valid distinction of characteristics of ethnicities among the different groups in the nation.

Differences that are as wide as any other all over the world of:

Language
Religion/Theology
Philosophy
Culture
Food
Traditional occupations
Arts and artifacts
Livelihood/aspirations
Dressing
Implements
Dance and Music
Physical features: size/shape/color/height.

Substantive Definitions, Objective or Subjective

The United Nations cannot decide that an African ethnic group could not dominate, subjugate, and enslave another African ethnic group. Emphasis on this is necessary because the classification of 'dominant' ethnic group's action comfortably mentioned: Australia, New Zealand, Europe, Americas and then an unidentified 'OTHERS'. Other listed qualities that must be satisfied are:

1. Self-identification as indigenous at the individual levels and 'being accepted' by the community as belonging to it.
2. Historical continuity with pre-colonial times
3. Strong link to territories and surrounding natural resources
4. Distinct social, economic, and political systems
5. Distinct language, culture and beliefs
6. Form a non-dominant group in the society

7. Resolve to maintain and reproduce their ancestral environments and systems as distinctive peoples and communities.

In countering the 6th item on the list, we must show that there is a lack of political representation and participation in the Nigerian contraption. There is active economic marginalization and a government's drive to impoverish the southeastern Nigerian ethnicities by Nigeria. There is a lack of access to social services and blatant discrimination against southeasterners so much so that they are deprived the product of natural resources in their lands through an unfair National revenue derivation and sharing policy.

So should Biafran nation be declared as enslaved and endangered indigenous people?

Political representation: Today in Nigeria (2015 – 2023), there are no easterner in the cabinet of the Federal government. There are no heads of any security forces of eastern origin. These are at odds with the present constitution, which as decreed and written by military dictators of the past, is manifestly unjust to south eastern Nigerians. Yet the little it affords the eastern ethnicities, are not followed.

Economic marginalization: The Nigerian government have refused to site any major industries or development concerns in south-eastern Nigeria. No seaports also, as Onne in Port-Harcourt and Calabar seaports are not allowed to operate. There are no international airports in southeastern Nigeria. Making international journey from eastern Nigeria costly, arduous and dangerous to south easterners.

Blatant discrimination: The existence of an affirmation policy that demands placement or employment or promotion, by selection of mediocrity over excellence have bastardized education and the civil service in Nigeria.

Why we need our core-experts in the relevant fields?

I am a soil scientist, so how would you expect me to delve into aspects of Nigerian impoverishment of indigenous Biafran ethnicities?
Where are our political scientists?
Where are the retired diplomats and lecturers who have relevant data and information?
Where are those who attended high-level conferences, who were affected by policies that were meant to kill Biafra?
Do you not realize that we need you?
I see many of you sit in judgement to criticize the work being done by those that are doing what they know and how much they can; to save the future of Biafra. Know that you have refused to lend a hand in controlling the focus of this our collective journey of self-determination.
Your titles are all in cards and books, your picture can only be recognized by your family, colleagues and friends.
Once you leave the safety of your home or office, the soldiers and all other security formation killing us, will shoot first and ask questions later. Know that you, as our strength and pride, is a formidable challenge to 'they' who would exterminate us, so you are not safe also; make no mistake about that. However, let us go on with this my analysis.
The International Labour Organization (ILO) in its 76th session on June 7th 1989, came up with a document: **C169- Indigenous and Tribal Peoples Convention of 1989**
This conference was based on the Universal declaration of human rights; the International covenant on economic, social and cultural rights; the international covenant on civil and political rights and many other international instruments with the aim of preventing discrimination.
After the convention, participants produced, a 44-article document primarily aimed at protecting indigenous people worldwide. Today 32 years later, only 23 nations have ratified those articles. None of

the five permanent member states of the United Nations ratified it. Only one country in Africa, (the Central African Republic) have. Only one country in Asia, (Nepal) have. Only Fiji in Australasia have.
In Europe, only those countries with best human rights records have ratified the document.
The rest are South American Nations, for whom ratification had not prevented from pulling back at the rights of indigenous people in their countries. Therefore, we cannot assume that Biafra is an easy venture to accomplish. For no matter how hard we struggle to push our case, unless we make it difficult to be ignored, we would not make any progress towards independence. The destiny of millions of Biafrans would remain impoverishment, marginalization and endless migration in search of peace and quiet to found a family and a home in foreign lands.

I want you to know that the text of the C-169 only demands:
"Consult indigenous people and establish means through which the indigenous people can freely participate at all levels of decision making, in elective and administrative bodies responsible for policies and programs which concern them"
The above three lines and its implications, are the reasons why indigenous peoples are subjugated worldwide. Their resources of any kind: natural, solid, underground or human resources are continually being dispossessed from them. They are systematically murdered, brutalized, some are forced to emigrate in search of a life they could have in their own lands (if they were left to fend for themselves).
This document is available online at: https://www.facing-finance.org/wp-content/blogs.dir/16/files/2012/01/ILO_169.pdf
Current affairs are panning out if you could remain focused on the action right now. Few months ago in one of my works, I explained that the United States of America was abandoning their war in Afghanistan because they are ready to commit for a war in Nigeria.

Within a few weeks after that write up, Mr. Anthony Blinken, the US Secretary of State, visited Nigeria and declared that there were no ethnic cleansing, no religious intolerance and no government or rogue actor's calculated attempt to annihilate indigenous people.

He did not say that? Ok, tell me what exactly he said!
Yes because I have some evidence we should peruse in the meantime.

1. https://twitter.com/uwanuruochi/status/1443952063612796933?t=KRUlYzeRVR0y7dvXTHH7ew&s=08
2. https://twitter.com/uwanuruochi/status/1446095448163323908?t=6wVev4MZ1Q2BGJEZ_jeOsg&s=08
3. https://twitter.com/biafra4ever/status/1446749222762688517?t=YxuU3Mrqi6f6MBYi376m5g&s=08
4. https://twitter.com/NBiafranblood/status/1446898510620774404?t=TpeG-cXiQq0Xmc1aQof08Q&s=08
5. https://twitter.com/VOCMediaConnec1/status/1447477803650256896?t=0ylWJiWgSs022Mn5OBMNpw&s=08
6. https://twitter.com/fa1a3dc63e584ba/status/1447821595146346497?t=770Czt0WhxzqWiWYMsJIMw&s=08
7. https://twitter.com/uwanuruochi/status/1450095309485273091?t=aqKg7l1-vTbTuaRym2nvmw&s=19
8. https://twitter.com/oduduwa_omo/status/1455328242886483972?t=279R17ktDmhisKOXVjkaXQ&s=08
9. https://twitter.com/NetworkBiafra/status/145561643643347353 6?t=bqMesZcwAvGJgLhcUVELKA&s=19
10. https://twitter.com/uwanuruochi/status/1443733750731325451?t=oeouqNgG2VgfDtAmiu3SrA&s=08
11. https://twitter.com/uwanuruochi/status/1443733750731325451?t=oeouqNgG2VgfDtAmiu3SrA&s=08

Let me tell you something, we need America, we need the United Nations to help us at least by speaking out for the incessant killings and strategic annihilations going on against indigenous ethnicities of Nigeria. We do not need them to support the continued genocide against us. That we do not need and we will say it.

A Perfect world

There will never be a perfect world NO! There will not be a perfect world. However, what we have at the present time, should not mirror biblical idea of hell because we are on earth. In the natural world we have all inherited, by virtue of being born into it, we would, as a matter of fact, bequeath same to our future generations.

All the inequalities that exists in our world today are just a function of the law of survival of the fittest.

There is only one law which mother earth gives to us, once our eyes opens to the reality of life and existence. The law of the jungle we call it. It is synonymous with every other region on earth because we say the earth is a jungle. Be it on desert landscape, the law of the desert, the law of oceania, the law in all of the lands and the seas across the earth is the same: **Survival Of The Fittest.**

Science thought of trying to reduce the impact of the implication of those very four words so they coined the essence of it into "NATURAL SELECTION." Have you ever wondered why the photographer will stand there filming while a Lion chases down and kills a perfect specimen of a deer, a wildebeest, a warthog or a buffalo. What of watching a baby animal being craftily separated from its mother by a predator; and torn to pieces even while it is trembling on weak legs that have not learnt to walk. All the while the photographers, their guards, lights and sounds personnel, cook and handy-man, just watches without intervening in any way at all. That is because, unless they were there to save a specific animal from extinction, letting nature move along its own pace is exactly how to ensure that both predators and prey and the inanimate physical world would survive from day to day. As it had done for millions of years in the past till today. The UN and all other nations on earth are photographers enjoying the carnage happening to native ethnicities in Nigeria. **However, they aid the Fulani nation who would in turn afford them access to the resources laid waste from indigenous lands. Where now is the principle of non-interference?**

So let me tell you Biafran leaders of thoughts, politicians of all divide, intelligentia, at home or in the diaspora. You are of Biafran extraction, and the genocide going on at home is of concern to you no matter how many layers of sand you, as the proverbial ostrich bury your head in. Maybe you have no wish to return to Africa, that makes no difference at all. Cover your ears with cotton wool, 1966 - 70 seeped in, this age will record its own history and in time you would realize that when you could had lent a voice, though, you remained silent. Remember just one single fact, genocides does not identify who among the targeted race/ethnicity to exclude. If you are part of the problem today, we will make you regret it tomorrow.

Stand up and demand we live, even as so we should; there is no shade to truth. No other ethnicity would leave their desperate conditions across the world in other nation battling their individual and specific circumstances to come and fight for you. Your voice and support may be all we need.

Evil can write articles

Save Biafran Souls Group

Biafran in Diaspora

Melaka Malaysia

7th October, 2021.

ATTN:

1) Joanne Kess

Special assistant to the President,

Univ., of Baltimore

2) Elizabeth Epps

Admin Assistant to the President,

Univ., of Baltimore

Dear Sir/Madam,

COMPLAINT AGAINST IVAN SASCHA SHEEHAN AND HIS ARTICLE "US IGNORES SMALL AFRICAN TERRORIST GROUP IPOB AT ITS PERIL" AND SUBMISSION OF EVIDENCES FOR A DETERMINATION OF THE EXISTENCE OF POSSIBLE ON-GOING GENOCIDE AGAINST INDIGENOUS PEOPLE IN NIGERIA

Introduction

I read with dismay the article identified above in Washington Post authored by a certain staff of your Institution Ivan Sascha Sheehan.

The meaning I derived was that the cloak does not make a monk or that this might be a case of money in exchange for useless research.

In producing an academic work, the author, supposedly a seasoned author, must be objective in his research because it is the result of the research that must proclaim the quality of work gone into the research and which in turn will carry the value ascribed to such details or data resulting from the work.

Academic degrees does not always translate to the quality of the person nor does it testify to the veracity of what the purported researcher comes out with.

There is what we term "peer-review" which in essence means that whatever an academic personality had produced will be subjected to the scrutiny of persons similarly qualified and in the field of study in other to testify to the veracity of the data and inference which the work so claims. Most work authored by columnists and some lecturers or persons who have laid claims to certificates fraudulently acquired had been published with a caveat: THE OPINIONS SO EXPRESSED ARE ONLY ...

What the caveat does is to absolve the publishing house of responsibility if they are later sued, or to give them a leeway out of claims of gutter journalism.

Now let me address the position taken by Ivan Sascha Sheehan in a recent publication in Washington post newspapers. A professor should value his title and not be available for purchase in exchange for money. Remember the case of Hwang Woo-suk in 2006. It was found that he had falsified data for pecuniary advantage.

Sometimes though, it needs evidence of facts and intention to prove that research had been tainted by character, lies, pecuniary advantage, wickedness and malice.

The Nigerian Biafra civil war 1966 to 1970 was fact.

United Kingdom, Russia, France, Egypt etc., supplied weapons and actively fought with Nigeria against Biafra, fact.

The Nigerian constitution presently is manifestly discriminatory against a section of its people, fact.

The Nigerian government has completely put in place a system to impoverish the southern states, which is exactly where Nigerian famed oil resources are. Fact.

You can also glean the truth of the Nigerian situation simply from infrastructural development caps and refusal to site any national industries, build roads, seaports and airports in the region, without conditionality, Fact.

Nigeria has gazetted itself into states that are deemed foolish by birth/ancestry and which indigenes must be accepted at zero scores in every venture in life, whereas the other zones must be accepted at not less than 70% in any determination for success. Incidentally the Southern states fall into the category that must achieve that 70%. Fact.

While the southern states aspire to join the rest of the world in the match to civilization, the Nigerian government had bought into the Boko Haram theory. Nigeria is actively engaged in wiping out the Christian minority communities in the Northern states and is using the Nigerian security forces now assimilated with so called repentant Boko Haram operatives to try to kill Southerners who are Christians. The result is that southern ethnicities have ignited agitation for secession which had reduced since after the Nigerian/Biafran civil war for equality and freedom to exist. Fact.

In the last ten years, the Nigerian army have carried out many operations termed "python dance", "crocodile smile" etc at which operations, thousands of southern ethnicities had been massacred for nothing, Fact.

Ethnic dichotomy, political differences, religious and ideological identities, cultural diversity and market realities are solid functions which determines the successes or failures of nation building. Iran is unsuccessful, Afghanistan is unsuccessful, and many more nations that you comfortably think are your examples are totally unsuccessful too. Fact.

The EndSARS protest barely a year ago took strength from the brutality of the police and army within this time, Fact.

The root causes of discontent, the background information, the voices of discontent, the method of agitation, the response of the Nigerian government and the position of the indigenous people who are at the center of this conflict, must form part of the theatrics for any discourses that seems to examine, research, project and determine what is going on in Nigeria. Fact.

Ivan Sascha Sheehan, who claims to be a professor have failed woefully in his myopic attempt to discuss what he has no idea of, regarding the case of the IPOB in Nigeria.

I have not the time nor the intention to educate you. The most difficult people to teach are educated illiterates among which Ivan have shown himself to be a major one. But in support of my appeal, I am herein presenting evidence which supports my assertion that Ivan Sheehan did not undertake any type of research before coming to the conclusion and publishing his article. Please be patient and open the very many internet sources, documents pictures and videos that are presented herewith. It plead also that you may furnish Mr. Ivan Sheehan a soft copy of this document. Maybe, in his deranged and psychotic mind, he may celebrate the killings and brutality they portray in abundance and maybe, these documents may cement his laughter in the reward he definitely had received to demonize a peaceful people suffering under the tutelage of slavery, inhumanity and genocide.

Your dreams of demonizing the most peaceful movement on earth will definitely fail completely. Across Europe and America IPOB, and it's sister organizations have continued peaceful demonstrations for more than ten years today. In cities across Germany, France and UK. In Washington, New York, and many cities across the world, not one single terrorist action have ever been linked or will ever be linked to us. Fact.

Yesterday, the 5th of October 2021, the Nigerian police shot and killed an operative of the Nigerian DSS who was carrying out deadly attacks against civilians in Imo state under the guise of Unknown Gunmen (- frame IPOB). Fact.

If you had done the slightest research, you would have understood what IPOB is and what it is peacefully agitating for.

But I doubt if your sponsors would have paid you a dime if you did a real work.

So I am reporting Mr. Ivan Sascha Sheehan to you for academic misfeasance, and impropriety. He should be told to please desist from his evil acts; even United States of America and United Kingdom know that you are fake.

Here below am sending to you a complete document with internet sources, which formed part of the Biafran's effort to attract attention in an effort to save itself from an ongoing genocidal campaign against it.

Following its Independence, Nigeria became a single nation with over 100 different languages, more than 50 distinct nations all completely different in every way: culture, language, dressing, way of life, religion, aspirations and physical features even. The nomadic Fulani herdsmen and the sedentary Hausa farmers, the royal kingdoms of Bini and other Yoruba nations. With village/town based Igbo clans where a village council (made up of family elders) independently govern their villages from time immemorial. (The first world known democratic system anywhere on earth). Thanks to colonialism and the 1914 amalgamation, they all must forge a single entity together with all other nations caught up in the vast area designated as Nigeria.

Biafra is a nation made up of about 10 ethnic groups in South East Nigeria. Biafra has an estimated population of about 40 to 70 million with about 40% of its people dispersed in the diaspora owing to the impossible situation the nation has found itself in the Nigerian contraption. In 1966, a group of Nigerian army officers launched a coup d'etat in Nigeria (two of the coup plotters were Igbo), Nigeria, thereafter selected an ethnic group "Igbo" for extermination. In the anger of the pogrom against southerners in the north and west of Nigeria, which killed estimated 20,000 to 30,000 southerners living in other parts of Nigeria. Southern Ethnicities joined and created Biafra to protect itself, the Nigerian nation fought them, with the help of then world super powers: United Kingdom, Russia, Egypt and Arab allies to annihilate the Biafrans.

In the light of the steady killings being perpetrated in Nigeria against The Indigenous People Of Biafra (IPOB) and against Christians. There have been repeated calls from inside and outside Nigeria. By members of Nigerian religious organizations, churches, Nigerian parliamentarians and Governors of states so affected. By International bodies too and we know in responsible ambassadorial reports sent to their governments. Nigerian situation is clear to the entire world. The government of Biafra in exile has been doing everything it can to get International attention. Yours truly have also written a detailed letters attaching pictorial evidence to the Under-secretary of the United Nations offices in Geneva, yet the calls of a declaration that there is possible genocide perpetrated by Buhari's government, by proxy 'bandits', 'vigilante' and by direct police and military forces has seemingly not been heeded by the United Nations.

Going by the United Nations convention therefore, we would assume that genocide means the intentional action to kill off a people entirely (usually defined as an ethnic, national, racial, or religious group) it does not matter whether the action is entirely successful or not, in so far as there was an intention and the action to produce the desired result.

According to the United Nations Convention on the Prevention and Punishment of the Crime of Genocide (UNCPPCG) Article 2.78 there are five main aspects that must be proven for a determination of genocide to be made:

1) Killing members of the group: The act does not enquire that the entire group be annihilated before genocide could be determined. Therefore, we ask the United Nations to please send in one of her officials to take up residence in any part of Nigeria, please bring a chair, paper and pen to continue counting with us. It is apparent that these several hundred thousand over the years are not yet enough for you. Or maybe you assume we are burying empty boxes by the thousands every week. Come and join us please send a representative to burry some of the boxes with us. This August week is ok! Come along, the Fulani has not finished with us yet.

2) Causing serious bodily or mental harm to members of the group: There are those torture method devised by the Army and presently in use in southern Nigeria. The first is to tie up the IPOB with their hands behind their backs and tie the legs similarly then arch the victim backwards, the victim is then hung on those ropes onto the rafters of the roof and a fire place is started under him. There is the second method of making their victims swim in and drink sewage or open drainage ponds. Flogging, beatings and anything that comes to their minds. Just open Facebook, these are entirely in the public domain. Filmed and posted by the men who are carrying out these atrocities.

3) Deliberately inflicting on the group conditions of life calculated to bring about its physical destruction in whole or in part: Nigeria has maintained a quota system through which Biafran progress is stifled. Stated as EDUCATIONALLY DISADVANTAGED. The Fulani and Hausa ethnic groups are the only race or ethnic group in the world who have branded themselves as being of a low mental capability and therefore must be accepted at as low as 3% passing scale to qualify for College admission. Whereas the Igbos and Biafrans and Yorubas must attain 70% to gain entrance to the same school, college or university in Nigeria. This is a complete lie and a disservice to itself. It demeans its human quality and is entirely responsible to the inability of the Fulani/Hausa races to hitherto attempt to compete fairly with other Nigerian ethnicities, had created mistrust and enmity and skewered meritocracy in Nigeria. Quotas are similarly placed in everything and this has stifled academic and professional development. Had affected the quality of manpower and is seen at every facet of national life. International relations are undertaken by officers who are not qualified but were appointed by quota system, contract negotiations usually are signed at the detriment of national interests because Nigerian negotiators are quota appointed whereas the country boasts the best level of experts in all fields of endeavor. Infrastructural development must be approved based on which region is allowed to develop or not. Today there are no good roads, NO operational seaports and NO international airports in Biafraland. Though it holds one of the largest oil reserve in Africa, Nigeria does not have a serviceable refinery, the country have to engage in deals that cost it the value of its natural wealth in other to export crude and 're-import' refined oil. We are ashamed, because local institutions, infrastructure and human skills and knowledge that would have been created and developed by concerted effort in the oil industry be it, (mining /refining /education /jobs /tourism) is lost. Military checkpoints are placed at

one kilometer distance all over Eastern Nigerian roads whereas the war against Boko Haram and other terrorist organizations are in the Northeast and North central of Nigeria. These infringes on the third Article II(b)of the Genocide convention, amounting to torture, cruel, inhuman, degrading treatment and punishment and all are being committed with the requisite intention to destroy ethnic Igbos and Biafrans and Christians in Nigeria.

History and position of the world to purported genocides

A few examples of known genocides carried out in the world are slave trade and conquest of Africa, Holocaust by Nazi Germany against Jews, the Armenian Genocide, the Native American genocide, the Cambodian genocide, and the Bosnian genocide, the Anfal genocide, the Darfur genocide, the Rwandan genocide. Wikipedia list of world known genocides included the Biafran genocide. "(1966 Nigerian counter-coup during which Johnson Aguiyi-Ironsi and Yakubu Gowon seized power, Aguiyi-Ironsi issued a unitary decree abolishing the regionalisation of Nigeria, leading to a series of massacres against the Igbo tribe, These massacres were hypothesized to have been organized beforehand,[367] and the Nigerian leadership later began to intentionally promote the extermination of the Igbo. The slaughter lead to the deaths of 8,000 to 30,000 Igbo, and resulted in the secession of Eastern Nigeria into the State of Biafra and the Nigerian Civil War.)" (1. 2.)

According to the texts of the UNHCR [7] "genocide does not necessarily mean the immediate destruction of a nation, except when accomplished by mass killings of all members of a nation. It is intended rather to signify a coordinated plan of different actions aiming at the destruction of essential foundations of the life of national groups, with the aim of annihilating the groups themselves."

We begin to wonder if the meaning we get from reading the above quoted text is exactly same as the United Nation Organization does. Especially when the document tries seriously to push the narrative that determination of the existence of genocide whether in the past or presently ongoing is a matter for academic exercise. The basic truth is that when there is an intention to wipe out entirely or in part an ethnic group, and then action carried out to achieve this purpose, genocide is determined to have been or is being committed. This is as simple as A, B, C. It is for the courts to make a ruling that such is the case in point. Why do we need to wait until half of the targeted group is killed off, before we need to take action? Watch it carefully! The times have drastically changed and the present crop of world leadership should be an indication of what is in store for the world in the present and nearest future. There was a time a single 15 cm hair-comb or let me use a better item, a Lady's facial-mirror would buy a sixteen year old British boy an entire town in Africa. Go and try it today! It was just about five years ago that someone who did not have what it takes to be a leader of the greatest nation on earth won an election on the basic truth (without its attendant finesse) of the dangers the world faced. Then everyone was toying with political correctness while he declared he wanted to MAKE AMERICA GREAT AGAIN; today we can appreciate how difficult the United State is finding it for having allowed the great lie in the first place. There is no safe haven for anyone again. Afghanistan created a generation of terrorists because the world allowed the problem to fester from a Russian invasion. It is still ongoing thirty years on and have spawn greater evils around the world: Syria, Iraq, Yemen and the genocide against Yazidis. You can argue that all these are discrete. I disagree because evil will always seeks a homeland. These terrorists need a safe haven from where to operate. Instability offers them that opportunity, but they come with their traditional hallmark of death and destruction. ISWAP is now in Nigeria. The case of the Islamic uprising in the north east of Nigeria started with a disgruntled colleague in a power tussle and metamorphosed to Boko Haram. Now it has given the leeway to ISWAP and has been drawn into an age-old hatred of the Igboman's skills and propensity to success. In Buhari the world saw a proxy leader, the type Britain wishes to have to keep Nigeria where it belongs: UNDER THE TABLE. We bet they did not wish for a genocide, but it was there all the while. He said it. There was the Boko Haram threat in existence. They chose him to be their Spokesman. He even demanded that the terrorists MUST NOT BE ATTACKED. In the meantime, he had declared: "DO EVERYTHING IN MY POWER AT ALL TIMES TO ENSURE THE COMPLETE AND TOTAL IMPLEMENTATION OF SHARIA IN NIGERIA!" So what was it we did not know? Nigeria is 55% Christians; tell me how you can impose Sharia in 100% of the country?

The United Nations General Assembly adopted the Convention on the Prevention and Punishment of the Crime of Genocide (CPPCG) in 1948 and furthermore declared that the "denial of the right of existence of entire human groups, shocks the conscience of mankind, results in great losses to humanity in the form of cultural and other contributions represented by these human groups, and is contrary to moral law and the spirit and aims of the United Nations" (22), so enforce the law.

The issue of reception by member states of the United Nations to the genocide convention would give us an insight to the workings of the world Body. The USSR then was opposed to the convention as it feared it may be caught in the webs of the convention because of its treatment of the many nations under the USSR 23.25 Other nations similarly sought to limit effectiveness of the conventions when it comes to extrajudicial killings they termed 'political.' By this it is implied, certain killings in our collective names MUST be sanctioned by our leaders without going through due process.

An African proverb says *"When crocodiles eat their young, what will they not do to the skin of a Lizard?"* what will Britain not do to Biafra, if they did not care for United Nations sanctions against them and a looming Gulf war in weaponizing Saddam Hussein against the world. It is high time the world should call for self-determination for Biafra. It has been more than 60 years following the Civil war yet Biafra had not stopped clamoring for self-determination. We purposely would not delve into the issues of mens rea or actus rea in talking about Genocide against Biafra and Christians in Nigeria. These have always been there right from Colonial times. In the first case we are not lawyers, secondly we are too incensed with the behavior of the world to rationally control 'myself' not to call you all manner of names and or curse you and all your generations inclusive. If Britain is honest to itself, of course it cannot (UK sold equipment for weapons of war to Iraq, when its own soldiers amongst other nations, were preparing to go to war against Iraq). Is there any more reprehensive behavior you can ever think of in the world? We challenge you to mention it here (Iraq affair "Arms for Iraq: scandal hits fan". The Economist. 325: 64. 1 January 1992. ISSN 0013-0613.) Of course Britain and Russia together with Nigeria fought Biafra in the 1966-70 war too. The United Nation should please ask United Kingdom what Biafra did wrong to them.

Another problem is that, maybe, the world is trying to push their narrow view in the Biafran case. There is the exclusion of social and political entities as targets of genocide. M. Hassan Kakar had said that the international definition of genocide is too restricted [66], and that it should include political groups or any group so defined by the perpetrator. "Genocide is a form of one-sided mass killing in which a state or other authority intends to destroy a group, as that group and membership in it are defined by the perpetrator," Chalk and Jonassohn.

Natural Resources

Nigeria at the present time must be seen for what it is, attempts to turn a blind eye to the injustices of Nigeria by the international community must be called out. Access to Biafra's wealth is major reason why many, especially among the ruling class, are seemingly content to let things remain as they are irrespective of the collapse of common sense and wisdom. Love is not holding this country together, crude oil is. If Nigerian crude oil were to run dry today, president Buhari will lead Northern delegation to UN to register an Arewa nation within 24 hours. Biafran war too was all about crude oil. The political establishment fears restructuring because of crude oil. So the factor of brotherliness and love has never been considered in our national history. Nnamdi Kanu, the leader of the Indigenous people of Biafra is boldly telling it as it is to the whole world, this may be irritable to those who are involved in the crime perpetrated against indigenous peoples. We know he is saying the truth but we hate him for the truth and secretly pretend to be holier than thou. It will do us a lot of good to quit this hypocritical life and purge ourselves the hate that have made us so vulnerable to tribal, religious and political manipulations. The leaders of Nigeria who make available to you the resources of their nation in exchange for political support and subjugation of their own people are not doing the right thing. The world whole-heartedly assume some innocence by pretending that 'your' gain of the resources of Nigeria stems from regular inter-national business negotiations. Such organizations know what we cannot prove but the lack of evidence does not absolve moral guilt in the death and suffering of generations of people who should be living better. Egypt, Assyria, Rome, Mesopotamia, Babylonia and many more are not here today even with the tremendous power they held at a point in history, so too, most powerful nations would one day be shadows of themselves. We are all sure of that and maybe because of this your stance on subjugation and oppression of indigenous peoples, our morale will grow, strengthening our resolve, empowering us, we would reach out and friends will come to our aid, weapons may become available, a brutal war will once again be let loose on Africa because we must be free. Do not remain silent for long.

Extraordinary Rendition

True to form United Kingdom effectively kept quiet of the whereabouts of its citizen Nnamdi Kanu who was thought to have been killed in the brutal attack of python dance 2. All other civilians and passers-by who were summarily brutalized and executed for being ethnic Igbo, were of course no concern to the world. 28 young men and companions of Mazi Nnamdi Kanu were executed at the home of Kanu's father, an Eze of his people. Eze Okwu Kanu, the Eze of Afaraukwu ancient Kingdom Ibeku Umuahia, and his wife died a few months after that terrible assault at his palace. So I would assume from your deafening silence even when they were unarmed law abiding citizens who were only demanding better governance. Surprisingly their sins was that they or their kith and kin were agitating for good governance prior to the time the army came in and started indiscriminate killings. The people killed on the streets of eastern Nigeria, could not even be called protesters. Because none was protesting at the time they were killed. They were killed while going on their daily activities.

Now the middle belt 'Christian minority' states of Plateau, Benue, Taraba, Zanfara, Yobe, Kaduna states and others are experiencing unprecedented killings.

There is growing unrests and attacks against indigenous people, while their political leaders dwell in greed and unrestrained political aspirations. This empowers and embolden the killer-Fulani herdsmen to attack and kill indigenous people knowing that the governors would not speak out against these killings for fear of antagonizing the president who is ethnic Fulani. (https://www.blueprint.ng/killings-ebonyi-indigenes-call-for-change-in-security-tactics/)

Here we would reproduce an exact report following a particularly brutal attack against indigenes of Ebonyi state. ["The Association of Ebonyi State Indigenes in Diaspora (AESID) has blamed Governor Dave Umahi, for the continued killings in the state. The Ebonyi indigenes said the recent attack is considered the highest number casualties in the South-east region in recent times. 'Natives' of the three affected communities were slaughtered in their scores with many dead and several others critically injured."

In a statement made available to Newsmen Tuesday in Abuja by the association's President Amb. Paschal Oluchukwu, expressed disappointment that "despite earlier signs and premeditations including an alleged audio voice note widely circulated on the Social media which alerted on the plan to launch a fresh offensive on our defenseless citizens, the Ebonyi state government took no action to protect and defend the victims of this recent onslaught.]

(https://www.blueprint.ng/killings-ebonyi-indigenes-call-for-change-in-security-tactics/)

Zamfara: It is difficult to put a figure to the killings. However, for a crisis that has spanned all of two years, the death toll is better imagined. Several hundreds have been killed in Zamfara since 2016 and hundreds have been buried in mass graves too. The modus operandi of the bandits are: they raid villages, tear down doors, drag the heads of homes from houses and hurl them into forests. In the forests, they establish contact with the families and demand a ransom. Once this ransom does not arrive on time, they proceed to killing their victims.

At other times, the bandits just kill for fun.

Victims of Zamfara killings have been buried in mass graves (Daily Nigerian)

The bandits also rustle livestock across villages and communities in Zamfara. Hundreds of cows, goats and birds have been forcefully taken from homes by rampaging bandits. From Ajia and Wonaka in Birnin Magaji local government, to Kayayi village in Shinkafi local government, from Yan Taskuwa to Kucheri, from Tungar Kolo to all the Kara markets in Zamfara, the bandits have left sorrow, tears and blood in their wake. The spate of killings in Zamfara has also prevented farmers from going about their business. As a consequence, food is becoming scarce in Zamfara.

What is being done by the government to stop the killings?

After indigenes of Zamfara State who reside in Abuja stormed the presidential village to register how displeased they are with the federal government over the killings, President Muhammadu Buhari issued a directive suspending all mining activities in Zamfara. Buhari said he is "constantly in touch with the security chiefs, and receive regular briefings on the situation in Zamfara and across the country. Let me assure that we will continue to do everything to motivate and equip them to respond effectively to all our security challenges".

But we are aware that Muhamadu Buhari and his security apparatus have no intention to address security effectively because the rampaging killers are his ethnic Fulani kinsmen. The police and military chiefs are similarly all ethnic Fulani. They would declare and make statements but that is all there is to it.

"Operation PUFF- ADDER" "OPERATION CROCODILE SMLE" but these have repeatedly been proven to be whitewashing the problem. In most instance, the military will offer no aids at all until the killer Fulani's attack then the military will go to stop reprisal attacks.

(https://www.pulse.ng/news/local/zamfara-killings-all-you-need-to-know/mbf1qrf).

State Approved Or Tacitly Supported Terrorism?

This is when a government through its policies supports and or turns a blind eye to terrorism. In Nigeria under president Muhamadu Buhari, there is no other way to describe the policies of the government but that there is a state approval of terrorism. We make no attempt to abridge or edit the report which we are placing here they are taken from newspaper reports at the time of the occurrences:

[The Zamfara State Government has earmarked a total of N200 million for its amnesty programme for 'repentant' bandits in 2021. The figure was contained in the budget details passed by the Zamfara State House of Assembly in December 2020. In a copy of the budget seen by Sahara Reporters, N354 million was also budgeted for projects related to grazing reserves.

The Bello Matawalle-led government had in 2019 entered a peace agreement with bandits, but the governor said negotiation with the gunmen is the best option for lasting peace in the state. Matawalle while hosting Mohammed Adamu, Inspector-General of Police; Yusuf Bichi, Director-General, Department of State Services (DSS); and other security heads on July 16, 2020 also offered bandits in the state two cows in exchange for every AK47 rifle surrendered. He explained that he chose to offer cows because the bandits need the cows to advance their economic interests.

In January, Sahara Reporters exposed how 15 brand new Hilux vehicles and cash gifts were given to leaders of different 'repentant' banditry groups by Matawalle.

“Those bandits have different group, so if they say they repent, the governor will give them a Hilux vehicle: but unfortunately they are now using the vehicles to carry out attacks," a military source told Sahara Reporters

"It's so sad, he called it peace and reconciliation programme, but all you need to be rich now in Zamfara state is to take up arms against the people."

Also, the state government recently granted amnesty to Auwalun Daudawa, the leader of the gang of bandits that abducted over 300 schoolboys in the Kankara Local Government Area of Katsina State. Daudawa and his gang on December 2, 2020 invaded the school, shooting indiscriminately to scare residents. The operation led to the disappearance of over 300 students.

The abduction happened when President Muhammadu Buhari was visiting his home state of Katsina. After their release on December 17, 2020, Matawalle, said the boys were rescued through the help of Miyetti Allah Cattle Breeders Association of Nigeria (MACBAN) and that no ransom was paid. Zamfara, like other North-West states, has in the last 10 years faced devastating attacks from armed bandits. A committee set up to investigate the menace of armed banditry in the region, headed by Mohammed Abubakar, a former Inspector General of Police, reported that in Zamfara State between June 2011 and May 2019, 4,983 women were widowed; 25,050 children were orphaned; and more than 190,000 people were displaced as a result of armed banditry.

Last year, Governor Aminu Masari, Matawalle's counterpart in Katsina State, said his administration had to pull out of the peace deal it had with bandits that had been terrorizing residents of the state. Masari said despite the peace deal, the gunmen continued to carry out attacks with their accomplices from Zamfara, Kaduna and Niger Republic, leading to "indiscriminate killings" and kidnappings in the state.] (http://saharareporters.com/2021/02/18/exclusive-zamfara-spend-n200million-%E2%80%98repentant%E2%80%99-bandits-2021)

Gunmen seized at least 136 students from an Islamic school in Tegina town in Niger state.

According to the owner of an Islamic school, no fewer than 136 students had been abducted from Tegina's Salihu Tanko Islamic School, Tegina town, Niger State Nigeria on Sunday 30th May 2021. Grieving parents are currently pleading with Nigerian authorities to step up efforts to save the students kidnapped by the gunmen. Meanwhile, a Niger state police spokesperson said the latest kidnapping was carried out by "armed bandits on board motorcycles in their numbers". The gunmen fired "indiscriminately and abducted a yet to be ascertained number of children", he said, adding that the gunmen shot one person dead in the process. Authorities said "tactical teams" have been mobilized to rescue the students, while a fighter jet was also flying over the area to try to spot the kidnappers and the abductees.

Mohammed Garba, the father of an abducted student while waiting for news about his child outside the school, said: "We want the authorities to do more,"

Meanwhile, Niger state's Deputy Governor Ahmed Mohammed Ketso ruled out any payment to the kidnappers.

Since December 2020, gangs of so-called bandits seeking lucrative ransom have kidnapped more than 700 students during raids on boarding schools and other educational facilities across northern Nigeria in several incidents.

Sheik Gumi an Islamic teacher have been involved in negotiations and payment of ransom to these criminal gangs. He had gone so far as to say that the bandits merited the ransom payments since they live in the bushes.

On Saturday, 14 students from a University in northwestern Nigeria were freed, after having spent 40 days in captivity.

In another related incident, kidnappers had freed 29 students abducted in Nigeria's Kaduna state after the parents of the students sold properties to raise up to 180 million naira in ransom money. This they paid to the bandits, there is reports also that some of the demands of the kidnappers included purchases of dozens of motorcycles for them. The readiness of the Nigerian security to curtail incidents of kidnapping and banditry comes into question; seeing that motorcycles are the bandits' preferred mode of transportation.

There is less security, and attackers have the opportunity to seize a lot of people, because they know that negotiating with the government will result in either amnesty or ransom being paid, meanwhile the Nigerian security forces are deployed to eastern Nigeria to kill and terrorize indigenous people who refused to hand over their lands to bandits.

At least $18.34m have been paid to kidnappers as ransom, mostly by families and the government, between June 2011 and March 2020, according to a report by SB Morgen (SBM) Intelligence, a Lagos-based political risk analysis firm.

Presidential Order to shoot and kill ethnic Igbo without reason

The "Operation Restore Peace."

The Inspector General of Police Usman Alkali Baba on Tuesday 27th May 2021, flagged off a new special operational action plan code named "Operation Restore Peace" supposedly for the stabilization of security in south East.

The IGP declared that the operation was aimed at confronting violence, proliferation of weapons and at the Indigenous people of Biafra and its armed wing the Eastern Security network. The transcript of his words has raised alarm bells in the region with the express understanding that the IGP is not sending the military to eastern Nigeria on any peace mission. He said: "Do not mind the media shout, do the job I command you. If anyone accuses you of human rights violation, the report will come to my table and you know what I will do. So take the battle to them wherever they are and kill them all. Do not wait for an order."

This is coming from a police force that have been accused of extra judicial killings, extortion and abuses that led to the SARS demonstrations last year; during which the police and army opened fire on unarmed protesters. This is coming from an inspector general of police who have offered no credible response to Boko Haram terrorists, bandits, killer-Fulani herdsmen and Islamic State West African Province (ISWAP) all of whom have claimed territories in Northern Nigeria presently.

This is a police that negotiates with armed mass kidnappers of hundreds of children not once, but repeatedly and whose military base in Zamfara state and Bornu state where both overrun and destroyed by terrorists.

Now he is sending the police and army to execute unarmed women, and children in Biafra land.

Abductions and killings are presently going on in Biafra.

Disturbing news have been reported from Abia, Imo, Enugu, Ebonyi and Anambra states, these reports are of Nigerian Army and police going from house to house, to markets and businesses and churches abducting innocent civilians engaged in their normal daily activities. A video show several instances of this disturbing practice at Izombe, Oguta in Imo state purportedly shot on 23rd of April 2021 (item 4, page 29). There was more than 10 military hilux-trucks in the patrol and the security forces abducted many youths, forced them into the trucks, and drove off. The individual who recorded the video reported that no reason was given for the abduction or where the persons are being taken to.

Another video shot on 18th May 2021 at Aba in Abia state, tell of soldiers and police arresting Igbo youths and giving the reasons that they have dread locks, was wearing torn jeans these arrested youths numbering about twenty were bundled into Hilux trucks and driven off to unknown locations.

At Akwakuma junction on the 15th of May, 2021, the individual recording reported that there were seven Hilux trucks, the police seized many youths to fill the trucks and those youths had not been seen since then, three days later.

At Umuonyeali Mbieri Imo state on 19th May 2021, the military again reportedly abducted youths with their three hilux trucks, there was no way family members would know where they are taking the abducted youths to, nor had there been any news of the youths taken away since these actions. With their tactics of intimidation, highhandedness and brazen trigger happy stance, the people are scared into submission, bundled into the military trucks and taken away.

Another video shared online shows the moment two policemen were trying to gain assess into a house with high fencing and heavy gates. Then one of the policemen put his rifle over the fence and repeatedly released several shots. This is in complete disregard to life of people and against every known legal principle of policing. There is no indication that these policemen were looking for any criminal or that any crimes have been committed in the first place.

Another more troubling news are the cases of releasing random shots all over the streets carelessly or deliberately targeting peoples' upper bodies. In Owerri on 17th of May 2021, a student was found shot dead and abandoned inside a roadside drain in a pool of his own blood all around him. Another student was warded

at a nearby hospital the previous day in the same area after she was hit in the arm by stray bullets while she was inside her hostel corridors. She reportedly did not even know that police were firing indiscriminately outside on the streets.
These are unprecedented and the governors of the eastern states have not done their duties as the chief security officers of their states to address these types of unwarranted police action.
Professor Nwaogu had in his twitter post roundly questioned the Governor's title as chief security officers of the state since they are unable to control state security. The United Nation, the United States of America and other well-meaning governments around the world should as a matter of urgency look into these matters.

Below is also a concise document produced by the Catholic Bishops conference of Nigeria after their 2017 annual conference.

[OUR HOPE IN DESPAIR: TOWARDS NATIONAL RESTORATION

A Communiqué issued at the End of Second Plenary Meeting of the Catholic Bishops' Conference of Nigeria (CBCN) at St. Charles Borromeo Pastoral Centre, Jalingo, Taraba State, 7-15 September 2017.

1. PREAMBLE

We, the Catholic Bishops of Nigeria, held our Second Plenary Meeting of the year at St. Charles Borromeo Pastoral Centre, Jalingo, Taraba State, from 7 to 15 September 2017. Having prayerfully reflected on the issues affecting the Church and our country, we now issue this Communiqué.

2. URGENT NEED TO ADDRESS GRIEVANCES

Our country is currently passing through a phase that is marked by tension, agitation and a general sense of hopelessness and dissatisfaction. This we believe is as a result of years of injustice, inequity, corruption, and impunity. There are agitations in many sectors of the country against the one-sidedness in appointments to key institutions and sensitive national offices, against marginalisation, and unfair distribution of resources and amenities. There are also allegations of cases of selective application of the rule of law.

In his inaugural speech as civilian President of Nigeria on 29 May 2015, the President sent out a message of hope and of his commitment to national integration and cohesion. He said: "Having just a few minutes ago sworn on the Holy Book, I intend to keep my oath and serve as President to all Nigerians. I belong to everybody and I belong to nobody. A few people have privately voiced fears that on coming back to office I shall go after them. These fears are groundless. There will be no paying off old scores."

More than two years later, the reality on ground and the verdict of most of our people across the nation – irrespective of religious affiliation, ethnic group or social status – point to the contrary. The inability of the Government to address the inequitable situation in the country has provided breeding ground for violent reactions, protests and agitations, which exploit the grievances of different segments of the country. We call on Government at all levels to urgently address these anomalies, remove everything that smacks of injustice, and give everybody and every part of our country a sense of belonging. We insist that merit and ability should be the primary criteria in making appointments and genuine needs the criteria for the distribution of amenities. We also urge the Government to be always sensitive to the multi-religious and multi-ethnic configuration of the nation.

As Catholic Bishops, we affirm that the legitimacy of every Government derives from its ability to listen to the legitimate yearnings and genuine cries of the people and honestly seek to address them. We therefore urge the Government at all levels to engage the aggrieved sections of the citizenry in a conversation worthy of a democracy. We are concerned that the deployment of soldiers in the midst of already restive youths could increase the nervousness among the populace with the potential of igniting a fire that could turn into an uncontrollable conflagration. On the other hand, we enjoin all aggrieved persons and groups to employ peaceful means within the framework of the existing laws of the land to express their grievances or even exercise legitimate pressure on the Government. Care must be taken by all to avoid actions and utterances capable of causing yet another armed conflict in the nation or any of its parts.

We demand fair treatment from those State Governments in the North that deny some of our Dioceses their rights to own landed properties for mission work by their refusal to issue them with Certificates of Occupancy. People of different religions need to co-exist, communicate, and be allowed to freely practise their respective religions everywhere in this country.

Furthermore, the other members of the political class in all the arms of government have, as a matter of urgency, to reduce drastically the immodest cost of running government in this country. If for no other reason, they have to do this as a sign of solidarity with most of their compatriots for whom the basic necessities of life – feeding, clothing, shelter, healthcare, energy, quality education – have almost become unrealizable dreams.

3. ARMED HERDSMEN AND THEIR THREAT TO SECURITY

The continued havoc caused by armed herdsmen in various parts of our country, can no longer be treated as mere clash between pastoralists and farmers. For apart from wanton destruction of farmlands and crops, some of these armed herdsmen are known to have laid siege on entire villages, killing, maiming, kidnapping, and raping. Besides, there are also reports that some of them are foreigners who have entered the country without proper checks by the competent authorities. Such persons are therefore to be considered a great threat to our national and individual security and their activities treated as acts of terrorism. We demand that adequate and prompt action be taken and be clearly seen to have been taken to stop their onslaught.

4. SOME LIGHT IN THE MIDST OF DARKNESS

Along with other groups in Nigeria, we acknowledge the modest success recorded in the ongoing fight against corruption, the substantial curtailing of the activities of Boko Haram, and the release of some of the Chibok Girls. We note the positive report about the economy gradually coming out of recession. Nevertheless, we expect the Government to put in place economic policies and strategies that will make positive impact on the lives of our people, thereby reducing hardship and advancing the socio-economic welfare of citizens.

We commend the vast majority of Nigerians for standing together and remaining law-abiding citizens in the face of many difficulties, challenges and even provocation. We condole with the victims of terrorism, natural disasters, conflicts and violent crimes, while we continue to pray for the deceased. The solidarity shown by many Nigerians to those affected by the recent floods that affected some parts of the country is a sign of hope for our common peaceful co-existence. We equally commend the assistance rendered by individual Dioceses and other humanitarian agencies to the displaced and distressed persons. We appeal to the Government to carry the Church along in the work of the rehabilitation of such persons.

5. NATION-BUILDING: A COLLECTIVE RESPONSIBILITY

Since the founding of our country Nigeria, too much attention seems to have been focused on "sharing the national cake" rather than on “baking that cake” by first building a strong and stable nation. The task of nation-building is a responsibility that rests on all the citizens of the country. We therefore call on all Nigerians to put more effort into working for the common good according to the principles of subsidiarity and solidarity. Individuals as well as smaller groups ought to have enough space for development while all contribute to the commonweal.

Irrespective of nomenclature, we sincerely believe that most Nigerians earnestly desire a truly federal system of government that enhances the welfare of all citizens. This would not only address the allegations of marginalization, but also make the fight against corruption more successful. Nevertheless, no matter what system of government we adopt, without a true conversion of heart by all and the readiness to make sacrifices for the common good, especially by persons in public office, we shall only be reshuffling our problems without solving them and shifting the epicentres of our national tragedies.

6. HIGH QUALITY EDUCATIOIN FOR ALL

As a Church, we reaffirm our commitment to the integral development of the citizens of Nigeria, especially through the provision of quality education. In this regard, we once more call on all State Governments to return to the old tradition by which Church and State collaborated in the provision of high quality education for all our citizens

We also enjoin the Federal and State ministries and departments of education to ensure adequate and comprehensive curriculum for Christian Religious Studies (CRS), in such a way that individual right to religious freedom and the right of the Church to teach and disseminate the Christian faith is not infringed upon. We totally condemn the so-called Comprehensive Sexuality Education (CSE) and dubious Maternal Health techniques that are not only contrary to divine law but also would encourage immorality. All health related programmes ought to show respect for the dignity and sanctity of human life, every human life, from conception to natural death.

We note with great concern the ongoing strikes among various members of professional groups in our country. We appeal to the federal government to honour all legal agreements with these organisations so as to limit the grave damage that is already being done to our society.

7. CHRISTIAN COMMITMENT TO NATION-BUILDING

In our journey towards national restoration, the role of Christians, the Clergy as well as theLaity, is fundamental. As priests, our commitment to Christ in our total and obedient self-giving to him through prayers and service of our brothers and sisters not only makes us grow in holiness but also contributes immensely to the restoration of our nation. While not permitted to participate in partisan politics, clerics are urged to foster among people peace and harmony based on justice (cf. Canon 287). The lay faithful, on the other hand, are expected and encouraged to bear witness to the Gospel in their private, public and political lives. In the words of Pope Benedict XVI: "The Mission of the lay faithful is... to configure social life correctly, respecting its legitimate autonomy and cooperating with other citizens according to their respective competence and fulfilling their own responsibility" (Deus Caritas Est,22).We therefore earnestly call on the Lay Faithful to intensify their efforts in bringing the light of the Good News to those places only they can reach. They are by their life of witness to bring Christ into the temporal order such as politics, business, and in their places of daily engagements (Christifideles Laici 42). By their vocation they are to challenge government policies that negate fundamental human rights and their individual and collective right as Christians.

8. THE MODERN MEDIA AS ALLY

We observe that modern media, especially social media, can be effective means of information, education and evangelization. We, however, notethat rather than tap their great potential benefits for expanding knowledge, many, especially our youth, have become exposed to such negative dimensions of the social media as organs for crime, the dissemination of hate speeches, slander,for peddling outright falsehood and misinformation. In these difficult times, we appeal to our people to be more circumspect and positive in the use of information obtained from and disseminated through the modern media.

9. THE MARIAN YEAR – PRAYING FOR PEACE IN NIGERIA

The Catholic Church in Nigeria declared the year 2017 a Marian Year, in honour of the Centenary of the apparitions of the Blessed Virgin Mary in Fatima, Portugal. We invite all Christ's Faithful to participate actively in this national celebration and to its solemn conclusion scheduled to take place in Benin City from 12 to 14, October, 2017. During this celebration we shall re-consecrate Nigeria to the Immaculate Heart of Mary. In doing so, we entrust Nigeria to the Blessed Virgin Mary, Queen of Nigeria, asking her to intercede on our behalf to stabilize the Nigerian ship of state. May she also obtain for us all the blessings and graces that we need as a nation. May she pray for us to attain peace in our hearts, unity, and tranquility.

10. GRATITUDE TO GOD FOR EVENTS IN THE CHURCH

We are grateful to God for the appointments, ordinations and installations of new Catholic Bishops in Nigeria: Most Rev Donatus AKPAN, ordained and installed Bishop of Ogoja Diocese on 7 July 2017; and Most Rev Hilary DACHELEM, ordained and installed Bishop of Bauchi Diocese on 17 August 2017. We heartily congratulate them and warmly welcome them into the CBCN. We are grateful to His Holiness Pope Francis for the appointment of a new Apostolic Nuncio to Nigeria, Archbishop Antonio Guido FILIPAZZI. We welcome him to Nigeria and pray that his tenure be blessed with a resounding pastoral and spiritual growth for our Church and the nation.

We thank the Holy Father Pope Francis for intervening directly to definitively resolve the crisis in Ahiara Diocese, which has lingered for nearly five years. We urge all the priests and the lay faithful of Ahiara Diocese to unconditionally embrace the paternal gesture of the Holy Father.

11. CONCLUSION: OUR HOPE DOES NOT DISAPPOINT US

We, the Catholic Bishops of Nigeria, do hereby make a passionate appeal to all our Christians and the rest of Nigerians not to lose hope. We may be traumatized but we shall not be broken (cf. 2Cor.4:8).We advise that Nigerians look at themselves and the country in a better light. Much cheering news abounds in the land amidst the suffering and hardship, the pain and the feeling of helplessness. We are hopeful that Nigeria will survive the present hardship and will become the better for it. "And our hope does not disappoint us" (Rom 5:5). We all are stakeholders in the Nigerian project. We must therefore work hand in hand with a better understanding of ourselves to build the Nigeria of our dreams.

We welcome back our President, Muhammadu Buhari, from his medical leave. We thank God who brought him back safely to the country to continue to work assiduously for the betterment of our land.

May our Lady Queen of Nigeria continue to intercede for us now and forever. Amen.

Most Revd Ignatius Ayau KAIGAMA Most Revd William A. AVENYA

President (CBCN) Secretary (CBCN)

Archbishop of Jos Bishop of Gboko]

This document above was from 2017, today the different bishops have taken a more robust stance against the government of Muhamadu Buhari.

[In a Christmas message delivered in December 2020, the Catholic Bishop of Sokoto, Matthew Hassan Kukah raised concern about what he called "**the much pain, sorrow and uncertainty**" in Nigeria. The revered bishop lamented the degeneration of the country, the apparent inability of government to deal with it and the levels of violence and bloodletting. He accused President Buhari of deliberately sacrificing the dreams of those who voted for him and embarking on a programme "to stratify and institutionalise northern hegemony by reducing others in public life to second class status." He further stated that Buhari was pursuing a self-defeating and alienating policy at the expense of greater national cohesion. In conclusion, Bishop Kukah pointed out that there was no way any non-northern Muslim president could have done a fraction of what President Buhari has done by his nepotism and gotten away with it. There would have been a military coup long time ago or we would have been at war, he concluded.

Bishop Kukah's Christmas message resonates across most of the country. Indeed, his message spoke the minds of most Nigerians who have continuously worried about President Buhari's utter disregard for national sensitivities and national unity. At no other time in Nigeria's history, except perhaps, just before the Nigeria-Biafra Civil War in 1966, had Nigerians questioned the basis of their co-existence. President Buhari, has by his actions and words shown contempt for the feelings of the various ethnic and religious groups that constitute Nigeria, leading to loud cries for national restructuring. Of course, there were a few voices, apparently beneficiaries from Buhari's rule that have characteristically, as they have done with other critics of Buhari, called for Bishop Kukah's head. A group, Muslim Solidarity Forum even called for Bishop Kukah to vacate Sokoto. Although the Presidency was to issue a statement reaffirming Bishop Kukah's right to live in any part of the country just like any Nigerian, that statement did not fail to add disingenuously that the tolerance of the Sultanate for people of all faiths aided Bishop Kukah's stay in Sokoto. What is clear however, this time, is that President Buhari's rule continues to divide rather than unite the country. Add this divisiveness to citizens' economic desperation, frustration and anger, and you have a country sitting on a tinder box.] (https://placng.org/Legist/bishop-kukahs-criticism-of-buhari-exposes-nigerias-divisiveness/)

Some links to video and pictorial evidence and Newspaper reports:

1. https://twitter.com/i/status/1399422832204042246

2. https://twitter.com/i/status/1398996743237275656

3. https://twitter.com/i/status/1398296097043320835

4. https://www.youtube.com/watch?v=sV2e2aGygbw

5. https://www.withinnigeria.com/gist/2021/05/27/video-man-in-tears-as-fulani-herdsmen-kidnap-his-wife-in-ogun/

6. https://www.facebook.com/watch/?v=1339690506229497

7.https://twitter.com/ChinasaNworu/status/1398996743237275656?s=19

8.https://pbs.twimg.com/media/E2xcDOQXEAMUCSi?format=jpg&name=4096x4096s

9.https://pbs.twimg.com/media/E2qhOJSXwAUlMe7?format=jpg&name=medium

10.https://pbs.twimg.com/media/E2qhOLtWYAscok-?format=jpg&name=medium

11.https://pbs.twimg.com/media/E2qhOKDXoAIrAef?format=jpg&name=medium

12.https://pbs.twimg.com/media/E2q3wELWYAIe1Xk?format=jpg&name=900x900

13. https://twitter.com/i/status/1399107176124256256

14. https://twitter.com/i/status/1399140075783421952

15. https://twitter.com/i/status/1399134390312226819

16. https://twitter.com/i/status/1399111680576131072

17. https://t.co/DwOD4e2g8Y

18.https://t.co/gomVfNy6yy

19. https://t.co/JjgWCtPXfU

20. https://t.co/8J2vIsSEO9

21.https://pbs.twimg.com/media/E2leYvYVkAUBypQ?format=jpg&name=900x900

22.https://twitter.com/i/status/1398573310712057857

23.https://t.co/RXyZw2tVnx

24.https://pbs.twimg.com/media/E2aaTtBUUAEqd5i?format=jpg&name=900x900

25. https://twitter.com/i/status/1397439983053467648

26. https://twitter.com/i/status/1397440545488658434

27. https://twitter.com/i/status/1397443873308246016

28. https://twitter.com/i/status/1397446967689547779

29.https://pbs.twimg.com/media/E2QR_SnXIAE4YCi?format=jpg&name=small

30.https://https://correctbn.com/breaking-we-acquires-ammunition-through-top-nigerian-army-officers-arrested-fulani-herdsmen-video/correctbn.com/breaking- we-acquires-ammunition-through-top-nigerian-army-officers-arrested-fulani-herdsmen-video/

31.https://punchng.com/we-know-those-behind-killings-but-havent-labelled-them-terroristskukah/?amp&utm_term=Autofeed&utm_medium=Social&utm_source=Twitter&__twitter_impression=true

32.https://twitter.com/odinakabiafra2/status/1400125451905949700?s=19

33. https://t.co/Azk7QSM6lG

34.https://twitter.com/SoludohDi/status/1400511501576904704?s=19

35.https://twitter.com/RaceEastern/status/1400542183363653633?s=19

36. https://dailypost.ng/2021/06/03/huriwa-drags-wike-before-international-court- over-threat-to-kill-bury-ipob-members/?amp

Ongoing Genocide

Sustained attacks and extra-judicial killings by the combined units of the Nigerian police force, Nigerian civil defense Corps and Nigerian armed forces teams and by armed killer-Fulani-herdsmen across eastern states of Nigeria.

On Sunday the 31st of May 2021, while the Biafrans were in somber mood remembering the genocide of 1966-1970 and the ongoing military killings sanctioned by Muhamadu Buhari, killer-Fulani herdsmen attacked more than 4 communities of Tologa, Odoken, Ndiobasi, and Obakotara in Ebonyi State killing over 30 people, women and children included. There were another 12 people in the neighboring state reportedly massacred at Ado Local Government Area of Benue state by the same killer-Fulani herdsmen.

Both Ado in Benue state and the communities attacked in Ebonyi are ethnic Igbos separated by state boundaries alone. Uchenna Okpokwu, a resident of the area said the invaders came with guns and matchets. There were graphic videos of bodies cut in pieces and several survivors with matchet wounds being stitched up in a hospital. Confirming the attacks the house of representative member representing the affected districts, complained about the latent inability of the security forces in halting incessant attacks against indigenous people by invading killer-Fulani herdsmen.

In Nwori community of Ebonyi state, pictures showed injured women and children lying helpless in a health clinic; they had matchet cuts to the head and all over their bodies and legs. An accompanying video related that several young babies were raped in front of their wounded mothers after their fathers had been killed. An injured mother showed a terrible anal injury in her one year-old child.

Similarly, suspected killer-Fulani herdsmen attacked Ekpoffo in Eha-Amufu community in Isi-Uzo Local government area of Ebonyi state and slaughtered four persons leaving another seven with serious injuries.

At Afor-Enyiogugu Mbaise five people were shot and killed by the police and army joint team. This news was taken from graphic video circulated online showing two bodies being hurriedly taken away in two different motorcycles for evacuation to a nearby hospital, another showed two victims with broken legs. Yet another video showed a victim with gunshots to his stomach being led away, for possible treatment, the rescuers were looking for means of transport to the hospital at the time the video were taken.

On Saturday 30th of May 2021, the Nigerian military responding to the order of the Inspector General of Police went to Owerri, to a hostel of the Imo state university and opened fire, killing about 15 students and abducting many more.

On the same day 30th May 2021, a video showed travelers fleeing bandit attack along Tegina-Zugero highway in Niger state.

In fact, therefore, we should try to point out, as have many others, what IPOB is. IPOB implies **'all' INDEGENOUS PEOPLEs OF BIAFRA**; constituting of all ethnicities found in the geographical area designated as Biafra. What is happening in Nigeria is not pogrom it has been ongoing since 1948 (Augustine Adah (2013-07-23). ["Will relocation of Tafawa Balewa LG headquarters guarantee peace?" Hallmark. Archived from the original on 2014-06-21. Retrieved 2014-06-21.)]. It is not to be equated as killing fields, it is full-scale genocide. It is a free for all. The government of Buhari, has allowed the influx of ethnic Fulani from all over West Africa into Nigeria for the singlar purpose of displacing indigenous peoples, promising the invading fulani's arms and unrestricted access to any part of Nigeria. *Harff and Gurr (1998),* defined genocide as the "promotion and execution of policies by a state or its agents which result in the deaths of a substantial portion of a group (72). May I ask the United Nations a question, what is the length of time Biafrans must live in a state of subjugation, afraid of which village would be attacked next? These are not short bursts of pogroms here and there from time to time. We can count from these online records.

Excluding cases of individuals or few person's killings that are not known or reported:

1953, Kano riot of 1953

Kano 1980 riot, Maitatsine, and Yan Tatsine

Masacre and riot 14 October 1991 planned crusade of Reinhard Bounike in Kano

Biafran massacre 1967-1970 All over Northern Nigeria estimated 30,000 killed

Asaba massacre 1967-10-07 Asaba, Delta State, estimated 5,000 killed

Odi massacre 1999-11-20 Odi, Bayelsa State

2000 Kaduna riots 2000-02-21 to

2000-05-23 Kaduna 2,000[9][10]–5,000[11]

2001 Jos riots 2001-09-07 to 2001-09-17 Jos Miss World riots 2002-11-22 Kaduna

Yelwa massacre 2004-02 to 2004-05 Yelwa, Shendam and Kano

Muhammad cartoons crisis 2006-02-18 Maiduguri

2008 Ogaminana massacre 2008-02-26 Ogaminana, Kogi State

2008 Jos riots 2008-11-28,29 Jos 381[17]

2009 Boko Haram uprising 2009-07 Maiduguri, Bauchi, Potiskum, Wudil

2010 Jos riots 2010 Jos 992

2011 Abuja United Nations bombing 2011-08-26

2011 Damaturu attacks 2011-11-04 Damaturu

December 2011 Nigeria clashes 2011-12 Maiduguri and Damaturu

December 2011 Northern Nigeria attacks

2011-12 25 Madalla 2012 Nigeria attacks

2012-01-05,06 Mubi, Yola, Gombi, and Maiduguri

January 20, 2012 Nigeria attacks 2012-01-20 Kano 185[26]

April 2012 Kaduna bombings 2012-04-08 Kaduna

June 2012 Kaduna church bombings 2012-06-07 Kaduna, Wusasa, and Sabon Gari

Deeper Life Church shooting 2012-08-07 Okene

December 2012 shootings in Northern Nigeria 2012-12-25 Abuja

2013 Bagamassacre 2013-04-19,20 Baga, Borno

Yobe State school shooting 2013-07-06 Mamudo government secondary school

Gujba college massacre 2013-09-29 Gujba Yobe school

Kawuri massacre 2014-01-11 Konduga Local Government, Borno State

Federal Government College Buni Yadi attack 2014-02-25

2014 Gamboru Ngala massacre 2014-05-06 Gamboru, Borno, Nigeria

Gwoza massacre 2014-06-02Gwoza, Borno, Nigeria200 300[44]
2014 Kano bombing2014-06-23 Kano, Nigeria

Zaria Quds Day massacres2014-07-25/26 Zaria, Kaduna State 2015

Baga massacre 2015-01-03,04,05,06,07 Baga, Borno

2015-2016 Killing of Biafran Protesters 2015-08-30 to 2016-02-09

2015 Zaria massacre

2015-12-13 Zaria, Kaduna State 700-1000

2019-05-21 Kaura Namoda, Zamfara State

2019-06-09 Maru, Zamfara State

2019-06-08 Rabah, Sokoto State 25 Kalhu, Tsage and Geeri villages in Rabah

2019-06-09 Satiru, Sokoto State 18 Satiru village of Sokoto state

2019-06-09 Shiroro, Niger State

2019-06-14 Shinkafi, Zamfara State

2020-04-18 Katsina State Mass murders and robberies in three locations.

2020-05 03,05 Plateau State 4 Messiah College High School was closed due to COVID-19,

2018-06-25 Plateau State 86 Christian farmers and Muslim herders

2018-10-19 Kaduna State 55 Christian Adara and Hausa Muslim youth

2019-01-16 Guma, Benue State Unknown Jukun and Tiv attackers

2019-01-28 Zamfara State herders Vigilantes

2019-02-04 Zamfara State villages in Zamfara State

2019-02-10,11 Kajuru, Kaduna State 141 (130 Fulani and 11 Adara) Fulani

2019 Kaduna State massacre:

2019-02-20 Ebete, Agatu, Kaduna State

2019-02-26 Karamai, Kajuru, Kaduna State 40 Adara

2019-03-02 Gwer West, Benue State 16 farmers Fulani herdsmen

2019-03-07 Bassa, Kogi State 20 Bassa Kwomu Egburra Mozum militia

2019-03-10 Aungwan Barde, Kajuru, Kaduna State

2019-03-10 Birnin Gwari, Kaduna State 17 Unknown

2019-03-11 Maro, Kajuru, Kaduna State 16-52 Adara

2019-03-16 Nandu-Gbok, Sanga LGA, Kaduna Sta

2019-03-17 Biase, Cross Rivers State 4 Ikwo militias

2019-03-18 Agatu, Benue State Several Agbaduma people

2019-03-19 Guma, Benue State

2019-03-19 Khana, Rivers State 5 Iceland group

2019-03-26 Jos North, Plateau State Christian and Muslim youth

2020-4-12 Tegina Kabata, Shiroro County Fulani herdsman

2020-10-24 Talatan Mafara LGA Zamfara state Bandits killed 20

2020-11-29 Bornu state attack Boko Haram massacre 40 farmers

2020-11-30 UN reports 110 killed by book haram in Bornu state

2020-12-10 Giwa LGA Kaduna state 30 persons killed by bandits

2020-12-16 Refugee camp attack 51 killed

2020-12-24 Boko haram burns church killed 6

2021-2-08 Kaduna attacked by bandits 19 killed

2021-2-10 Sabuwa town attack katsina state 13 killed by bandits

2021-2-11 Kaduna state attack 23 killed by assailants

2021-2-25 Igabi LGA kaduna state 15 killed by bandits

2021-3-1 Illela Amarawa Illela LGA Sokoto state 12 killed by bandits

2021-3-2 Zamfara state Herdsmen attacks 40 killed 80 women abducted

2021-3-6 Sokoto attacks 15 killed by bandits

2021-3-19 Kauru LGA Kaduna state bandits kill 13 injure 7 burn 56 houses

2021-3-31 Egedege and Eha-Amufu towns Enugu/Ebonyi state boundaries 16 killed by herdsmen

2021-4-01 Chikun, Giwa and Kajuru LGA Kaduna state 18 killed by bandits

2021-4-6 Kibiya Kano state 9 ethnic Igbo Christians killed

2021-4-5 Yewa Ogun state Fulani herdsmen 55 killed

2021-4-9 Benue Monarchs palace set on fire 30 villagers killed by Nigerian army

2021-4-10 Mbator Shangev-Tiev Konshisha LGA Benue state 40 killed by herdsmen

2021-4-22 Magami LGA Zamfara state 50 bodies recovered

2021-4-23 Magami attacks Zamfara state 60 more bodies recovered

2021-4-24 herdsmen attacks: Ekiti state 6, greenfield university Kaduna 3 students killed.

2021-4-26 Boko haram sacks army base 30 soldiers killed

2021-4-28 Dadu village Benue state 8 killed by herdsmen

2021-05-09 Shadadi village Mariga LGA Niger state 8 killed 100 kidnapped

2021-05-13 Ozubulu Anambra state Fulani herdsmen 20 killed

2021-5-19 Assemblies of God church Kaduna Fulani herdsmen 8 killed

2021-5-19 Gwer west LGA Benue state Fulani attacks 4 killed

2021-5-24 Agan council ward Fulani attacks 9 killed

2021-5-19 Katsina-Ala Benue stateattacks 36 bodies recovered

2021-5-21 Fulani attacks Benue state 42 killed.Kaduna 10 killed Taraba 14, Zamfara 11 killed

2021-5-20 Benue Fulani herdsmen attack 42 killed

2021-5-27 Izzi LGA Ebonyi state Fulani attacks 30 slaughtered

2021-5-29 Ebonyi and Benue states Fulani attacks 46

There are very many attacks not covered in this account, especially cases of less than 3 deaths or where we were not sure if the case had been included in general recorded tabulation 2020. Similarly, many mass school kidnapping cases not captured in this report because those were always reported in the CNN, BBC and Aljazeera and other media when they occur.

Our Prayer:

We therefore call on the United Nations to explain to Nigerians of different ethnicities how to exist and make any kind of life in this type of insecurity. The world is still reeling from the Arab spring and the mass emigration it created. Is West Africa ready for the influx of new refugees? Is the world planning to starve out the Biafrans as they did in the 1960's? You must listen to your own staff on the ground or allow Biafrans an ear to air their grievances to make a concise case why they seek self-determination. It is high time we were invited to the table. An Igbo adage says *"Ebe nwata na akwa-akwa n'aru aka ma Nneya anoghi ngo, Nnaya no ya"* meaning

WHEREVER A WEEPING CHILD IS POINTING AT, THERE LIES IT'S SURVIVAL LINKS. We have wept for so long, we need to come home and rebuild our scattered homestead. We need to return and rebuild our towns and cities that had been so crudely desecrated by war and wickedness. We need our homeland back from Nigeria and her enablers, so we can live free and proud as a people in our own homelands.

We had hope in President Joe Biden, who had been in political office for most of his adult life, to look into our plea for a dying race of people so badly used by the world for the simple fact that our land is rich in mineral resources. But he failed us woefully.

We have no hope in Antonio Gutteres, the United Nations chief, because we have written severally to the United Nation Organization without any acknowledgement of receipt to our pleas, both to UNHCR, the African Office, and the Hague for three years today. Yet the fact remains, United Nations owe ethnic Igbo a listening ear, as we are also part of the peoples of the world. We call on all peace loving Nations of the world not to forget us. Finland is a nation we shall always be proud of. Someday Finland would be happy they did not turn their backs on us. To the state of Israel, rightly or not, there are basic resemblances to our traditional cultures, which are intriguing to all who study both our civilizations, do not let us die out. To Russia; you fought against us in 1966-70, we believe that by now you would have come to a better understanding of who we are and be ready to judge us correctly. To Germany and France, and Italy, we are 99% Christians. For all our faults we live in your homes and nations, have married your sons and daughters. If we are so evil, you would not allow us to live among you, marry your sons and daughters, work and contribute to your economies. Thank you Norway, thank you Portugal, thank you Spain, thank you Switzerland, thank you Belgium thank you Rome, thank you Netherlands. But we are still at war with the entire world for our survival as a people. We are still appealing for your consideration and a kind word for us among the comity of nations. To China, we hope that your rising power would be exercised with due diligence, even though you have a culture of hatred which you showed clearly by expelling innocent Africans from hotels and homes they legally paid for, during the Covid 19 pandemic. Canada and all the Nations of South America we humbly ask you to put in a kind word for us too.

We have attacked no one, we have not campaigned against anyone, we do not carry weapons of war, unless in self-defense, as we are able to realize our dreams without recourse to subjugation or displacement of another.

Amongst our brothers and Sisters are many who entertained you in the field of sports, Kanu Nwankwo, among so many other renowned footballers, Chinua Achebe, Emeka Anyaoku, former secretary of Commonwealth. Phillip Emeagwali the father of Internet and many more. There is no need to list names, for amongst every TEN AFRICANS YOU SEE on your streets anywhere in the world, at least more than SIX of them is an ethnic Igboman. You know us very well. Let us have our own homeland and stop perambulating the whole world like outcasts on the face of the earth.

Finally, Mr. Prosecutor of the International Criminal Court, the world have given you this duty because you are equal to the task give us justice we pray.

Thanks for your good offices,

Yours faithfully,

1. Uwanuruochi, Augustine. (M.Sc Soil Chemistry and Mineralogy MOUAU- Diasporan Ethnic Igbo based in Malaysia)

2. Oluchi, Gerald Ibe (M. Phil. History – Diasporan ethnic Igbo based in United State of America)

3. Professor Dr. Mrs. Maureen Eke (Ph.D Comparative Literature Indiana Univ. Bloomington. Diasporan ethnic Igbo based in United Kingdom)

PS. Definitions: Biafra was used regularly to include all the ethnicities of the indigenous peoples of Southeastern Nigeria and the entirety of the same group that seceded from Nigeria following the genocide of May 1966-1970.

Sources:

1. UN General Assembly, Convention on the Prevention and Punishment of the Crime of Genocide, 9 December 1948, United Nations, Treaty Series, vol. 78, p. 277, available at: https://www.refworld.org/docid/3ae6b3ac0.html [accessed 4 June 2021]

2. Convention on the Prevention and Punishment of the Crime of Genocide: Approved and proposed for signature and ratification or accession by General Assembly resolution 260 A (III) of 9 December 1948 Entry into force: 12 January 1951, in accordance with article XIIIhttps://www.ohchr.org/EN/ProfessionalInterest/Pages/CrimeOfGenocide.aspx

3. (https://ocdn.eu/pulscms-transforms/1/lLTk9kpTURBXy8yYjA4YmZjNjE4NDdkOGIwYTczNjViNjNkZWUxYWQ1Ni5qcGeQgaEwBQ)

4. https://www.amnesty.org/en/latest/news/2015/06/Nigeria-Senior-members-of-military-must-be-investigated-for-war-crimes/#:~:text=More%20than%201%2C200%20people%20have%20been%20extrajudicially%20executed,had%20fled%20Giwa%20barracks%20after%20Boko%20Haram%20attacked.

5. https://www.amnesty.org/en/latest/news/2020/06/nigeria-horrific-reign-of-impunity-by-sars-makes-mockery-of-anti-torture-law/

6. BAZÁN, José Luis, Fulani militias' terror: 2017-2020, Working Paper, Brussels, 16 May 2020 WORKING DOCUMENT FULANI MILITIAS' TERROR: COMPILATION OF NEWS (2017 - 2020) José Luis Bazán Ph. D. International Law Independent Researcher and Analyst, Brussels (Belgium) Contact: hispanialex@yahoo.es Website: https://independent.academia.edu/

7. https://www.anaedoonline.ng/2021/06/02/latest-president-buhari-threatens-igbos-with-second-civil-war/

Articles and news magazines of the times: Nation Building from within

Ndewo nu Umu Nnaa, obu Iwunna bia kwara ozo n'ututu a.

It shall be well with us all, the day which have opened its doors to the blazing rays of the sun shall filter the glory of Chukwu Okike Abiama into your homes today, (Kweerem Iseeee!!!!). **Iseee!**

You shall be fruitful and successful in whatever you truthfully engage in for your daily bread! **Iseee!**

The waters, the air, the soil and the forests shall respect your wishes! The Earth and the heavens will favor you! Biafra shall be free! **Iseee!**

The eyes of the evil man or evil woman, at work for ages shall never see you! The path of your life's journey today shall be in front of those that pursue you and they will never overtake or draw near to you! **Iseee!**

We live in the natural World; we must realize that we are mere mortals limited by the natural laws of nature. One of these laws imply that as flesh and blood we feel, we bleed, we are limited by time and by the totality of physical power we can muster as individuals, and we can also die. But then, we have the ability to think, to plan, to strategize and to create by an incremental process something that would marvel the entire world. We can be patient too.

Throughout human history those who have been able to make changes, small or large to human existence and experience, have done so in response to articulated reasoning, timed operation and systematic engagement. In the end, our journey as individuals cannot be extricated from the journey of our ethnic group, our race or our nation, so that with the failure of everyone also comes the failure of ONE. However the failure of ONE, even though may not mean the failure of all, apparently delays the progress of all. Assuming that a tribe caught in an ongoing flood event, decided to move out of their natural enclave to higher grounds. But because geographical constraints, must scale a smooth cliff edge, which none among them had scaled before. One of them, a radical and burly fellow, who had made a name for himself in not towing the 'common-line' before, but is well-liked, adventurous, wiry and resilient goes first. Everyone watches and gives him support, near the top he makes a fatal mistake and falls. The people watch in horror many run in to help, all efforts provided to resuscitate him fails. The flood is still raging; the cliff side is still standing against the tribes escape to higher ground. The tribe as human as they are cannot stop at all, another must go up again and again and every help must be provided to these heroes again and again.

Chukwuemeka Odumegwu Ojukwu is that first giant who tried to help us escape "the flood". Uwazuruike, Mazi Nnamdi Kalu and the totality of individuals and organizations local and in the diaspora are our second assault on that cliff side surface.

Abhijit Naskar wrote that the rise and fall of a nation are both predicated not on the actions of its government but those of its citizens. As I said above, we can only summon so much physical force as individuals or as a part of the whole, but as the whole or 'all' there is no limit to what we can do.

I am bringing to you today "nation building from within."

A nation can be said to be a group or race of peoples who share history, traditions and culture, maybe religion, maybe language too. United by a central government and a national Identity. Many nations of the world went through great upheavels in other to exist as a single entity. Those periods are fraught with the difficulties of blending them into being able to adopt a unified structure and this would have involved negotiations: peaceful or violent. In the much distant past violent negotiations were the norm. In the world as it is today, violent negotiations are options but nation building are finally decided across a round table. South Sudan from Sudan and Timor-Leste from Indonesia are examples. We are seeing very many violent negotiations raging around the world today. These are occurring at their right time following disruptions to natural march to civilization by colonialism. These 'forced-independent' contraptions have found out through half a century of existence that they cannot exist as an entity. They may be are too large, have too many differences within and between its component regions owing to the arrogance of colonial demarcations.

Ambazonia in Cameroun, Biafra/Oduduwa and others yet to emerge in Nigeria, Tigray in Ethiopia and many others across Africa and Asia. Some of these negotiations are at very early stages but you can identify such future conflict zones by looking at the reasons for lack of progress, and their lack of a national direction.

Bad governance, uncontrollable corruption, recurring religious conflicts, lack of a political direction, proliferation of personality cults and a country that is largely un-empathetic in its national psyche are signs of failing nationhood. These signs precede the outbreak of violent negotiations. Violent Negotiations are sad to say signal to the third phase of nation-building.

Most western writers in their work about nation building, prefer to hide behind verbose descriptions of simple principles, in other to deceive themselves and you. An example is the work of Almond and Coleman. They described two principles they called input functions (Political socialization, interest articulation, interest aggregation and political communication) and Output functions (rule-making, rule application, rule adjudication) as being important factors to nation building.

Basically, what I see is the lack of a unity of purpose arising from varied cultural and political consciousness, undefined sense of purpose because of conflicting traditional and religious beliefs.

These two factors encompasses and defines every difficulty you can think of why many colonial nations failed, are failing and will continue to fail. Zimbabwe a case in point, South Africa will fail too and as in the case of Nigeria, South Africa poses a great catastrophe to the world. The United States of America is not a good example to the world at the present because unless you look closely you may not easily identify the features I am describing in this study. But for your enlightenment; the primary question is to ask yourself: what does Trump stand for in your opinion? Did you see the signs of a personality cult? Did you see diverse opinions where truth and fairness did not matter? Think of institutional subjugation of certain races for the benefit of another race and the lies that such a practice does not exist being upheld by Trump's people in the USA and think of the attempted use of Police and the military to suppress existing freedoms.

I shall not digress here.

It is important to note that failing states would do all in its power to hold on to a dream which favor the benefiting class or ethnicity, therefore existing political systems cannot afford the majority a pathway to self-determination. In most cases, the involvement of an external superior power will be able to control nation-building efforts for the benefit of the different ethnicities in a failing state. The case of Sudan is a point of reference. The United Nation provided a platform for a separation, but this is a rare situation. United State involvement in Vietnam still did not end with a strong state. In Korea, the conflict is still ongoing. Afghanistan is a present hot spot and the United state is trying to pull-out of Afghanistan because they want active participation in the Nigerian-Biafra conflict engineering itself right now. Read in between the lines, what I know is that if they fail to learn from their experiences these many decades of wars, they may be caught up in wars forever.

There must be a unity of purpose for a nation to stand. There must be a shared direction in governance or in development for the peoples of a nation, the shared purpose must be rooted in culture, religion and tradition. You cannot force principles into or out of a people, not even with a gun or a grenade. Especially when United States enter these conflict zones, there is talk of "interests." Now which interests are important in conflict zones if there must be an establishment of peace. Remember that peace at all cost means no peace at all. That is why Iraq and Libya are still not at peace with themselves. Let us glance at the situation in Lebanon. In 1982 two of my classmates in secondary school were children whose parents left Lebanon following the war. Today Lebanon still know no peace because the system the world created for them is unworkable. Use my chart to identify the marks of a failing nation in Lebanon. Lack of a common national direction, very wide social/cultural/religious heterogeneity, widespread corruption, bad governance, existence of accepted personality cults.

Someone wrote: ‘a nation is not defined by its borders or the boundaries of its land mass, rather a nation is defined by adverse people who have been UNIFIED by a cause and a value system, and who are committed to a vision for the type of society they wish to live in and to give to the future generations to come.’ Read this quote carefully, you can identify that the source of their unity is a common cause, and the commonality is rooted in culture, religion or tradition.

In the world of today, there are acceptable human rights standards which people across the world expect to enjoy and this have made it impossible to impose external will of imperialism on weaker nations.

The failure of the United Nations in helping to bring peace to emerging nations is encased in the LIE that nation building is all about money, building streets, cities and setting up large armies. That is what the United Nations and United State of America and their allies have been doing in over fifty years of involvement in the creation of new nations following violent negotiations. There had not been an attempt at dividing these nations at the lines of least resistance and then allowing the nations to re-build themselves up again.

Ambazonians are English speaking areas of Cameroun, they make up less than $1/10^{th}$ of the land area of Cameroun. Any negotiated settlement that seeks to grant autonomy to the English speaking area of Cameroun will specifically end the armed conflict. Especially if you realize this particular region was forcefully merged with French Cameroun in the years between 1950’s to 1960’s through a sham referendum and agreement between the colonial powers Britain and France.

The United State and the United Nation would instead send in an army and sit in between both nations for as long as they want in the meantime milking the nation dry and setting up rival gangs who would continue warring against each other therefore, creating a sham "necessity" for the foreign forces to remain in disputed territories. At whose expense? They do not negotiate a division at all, then, after about ten years, the troops would be pulled out and both sides of the conflict would re-engage each other all over again. Afghanistan on my mind. Biafra have clear lines of demarcation what we want is to live free and not under economic bondage, educational bondage, travel bondage, developmental bondage as opposed to the freedoms granted by a failing UN.

A work by Simon Ekpa, in one of his broadcasts compared nation states of Europe to regional areas and states in Nigeria.

If you drive at 110 kilometers per hour from Paris in France right through the entire nation of Belgium; and continue onwards to Berlin at the north-eastern end of Germany; that is the same distance and time it will take you to drive from Umuahia in Abia state to Ojota in Lagos state at the samespeed and time. That is 9 hours at 110 klm/hour. If you assume this distance is not far enough, I will give you an idea of the differences in the traditions of the people. Consider that you have traversed lands owned by at least 20 to 30 different language groups, different religious affiliations, different cultural identities and different outlook to life in these areas we just zoomed in. France as a nation is made up of only four ethnic groups Basque, Flemish, Walloon and Celts. Belgium has Danes, Frisians, Roma, Sinti and Sorbs. Germany has only one ethnic group German.

Do not be pushed into trying to defend any perceived opinion of yours for a contrary view. For these people are not as stupid as we are when it comes to nation building. I do not want any 'ONE NIGERIANIST' to say Four Ethnic groups? Or Six ethnic groups? In a perceived false claim that there is a similarity in what British amalgamation sought and is enforcing in Nigeria.

In these three nations I am using as an example, there is a complete unity in terms of a national identity, national direction and national purpose to excel and to create a worthy society for its peoples and its generations yet unborn.

Let me zoom into Germany. The nation of Germany is divided into 16 states, each state has its own CONSTITUTION and remains FAIRLY AUTONOMOUS. Despite its large population, Germany has relatively few large cities, and only four cities in Germany have a population over 1 million people living in them: Berlin, Hamburg, Munich and Cologne.

Zoom in to Lagos: as at 2016, it has a population of 7.938 million people. That is exactly 8 times the most populated city in Germany,

It is so diverse that during electioneering campaign in 2015, the yoruba Oba threatened that Igbo ethnic group would be driven into the sea and drowned if they vote in opposition to another ethnic groups choice. In Lagos, the Fulani ethnic group enthroned an Emir, seeking to upturn century old traditional government system of the Yoruba-Oba kingdoms into Fulani/Hausa emirates. The different centers of excellence in Lagos are now being threatened for being Igbo owned, even when the lands were purchased through normal legal transactions, developed according to State housing plans and had been approved as at when the approvals were given by the department of lands. Can there ever be a clearer example of a failure of nationhood due to disunity in collective direction. These few differences I have mentioned above stem from cultural and traditional ideology, traditional principles and societal life outlook, which differ radically among the many peoples of Nigeria.

Nation Building demands a defined purpose. Where the anthem, colors of state, national pledge and the flag are accepted, promoted, celebrated and encouraged by the peoples of the nation without duress. This collective identity engenders collective aspiration that the majority of the peoples of the nation upholds.

Without mincing words, we are aware that a house divided against itself cannot stand, so why does the United Nation expect Nigeria to stand? Is that not complete hypocrisy?

In fact any one from whichever organization who tell you, Nigeria can be workable is part of the major problem. Because THERE IS NO WAY NIGERIA CAN WORK AS IT IS STRUCTURED. Unless the different flags that are opposed to each other, are allowed to fly within the whole entity, are allowed to pursue their own constitutional aspiration within the whole entity and allowed to develop in line with her own "collective-ethnic" based agenda in the framework of its territory.

Not to pull Igbo spirit of development into Kano and impoverish Igbo homelands by forced political policies and economic marginalization.

The Constitution

A national constitution is a document, which unites a diverse population by setting out common ideals and values. It creates a collective identity to bring its members under mutual or shared values, so that all who commit to that constitution are assimilated into a union. A national constitution should grant equality to all its citizens, set out basic rights granted to every one under it. It creates a commitment to provide for the wellbeing of all its citizens no matter their socioeconomic status, age, religion or ethnicity; giving each individual freedom and opportunity to establish themselves within a maximum ambit of the law.

Do you now understand why every state in Germany have her own constitution? Because today the German peoples are united under one ethnic identity as Germans. Yet from time immemorial,

Germany descended from very many ethnic groups over thousands of years in a fluid system of conquests and re –conquests when the march of civilization was in infancy. Phoenicians, Slavs, Assyrians, Barbarians, Romans. Though Germanic people themselves have collectively attained a complete mix assimilated as German; yet they need a constitution for each and every state. What does that tell you? Nigeria does not have such a constitution therefore is not a nation per se.

Do not try also to hold onto an assertion that Nigeria is young in comparison to Germany. No! Man as we see him today, homo-erectus came out from Africa according to overwhelming accepted research study.

When you are in the diaspora, you see things differently from your friends and family in the homeland. To start with, there is nothing wrong with the way people do things in their native homelands. As a matter of fact, expediency, trial and error, natural conditions at home had over time informed the method and systems people live in their homelands. After all Igbos say: "*Nku no na mba na eghere mba nri* meaning, (the wood found in foreign lands are what they cook with) behavior is affected by territory.

Secondly it is exceptionally true that wherever you consider a diaspora, is someone's homeland.

Therefore the question arises, who is to say that someone's homeland is better in all ramifications in comparison to another someone's homeland. The answer to the above question is very simple. Natural wisdom and knowledge had always progressed through an incremental process, acquiring experiences modelled by circumstances and reasoning as time and knowledge increased.

Let us look at this analogy; there is no cold weather (round the year temperature less than 18 degree celcius) in Southern Nigeria therefore fur coats, woolen sweaters and jackets could never had made any sense to us, may never had been thought of, created or needed by someone from eastern Nigeria, who lives in eastern Nigeria. However, survival of the fittest had always been the norm in tropical Africa, therefore the development of a legal system, which allowed safe living, enforced respect to one's tribe and peoples by creating order based on equality; meant that the tribes and ethnicities did not wipe each other out. That came out of Biafra.

The fact is that while we hid in our forests, claiming to be self-sufficient, marauding tribes had the run of the world. They swamped their neighbors, stole the laters' wisdom and thought, borrowed their systems and methods, displaced more tribes, used art and crafts they did not invent and went from place to place, from land to lands using collated wisdom on their way. They depended on crafts that never existed in Europe convinced neighboring tribes to reveal secrets of each other in the Americas, Asia and Africa and in the Oceania. These marauding tribesmen used your knowledge to enter your next-door neighboring village. Convinced you to bear arms you had no knowledge about and exterminate another tribe with whom you had shared the homeland for centuries.

To this day, your ancestral arts and crafts are in London, Germany, France, Belgium and all over Europe and you still believe that there is nothing you could learn from the diaspora?

Your sons and daughters are in the diaspora. They have lived, grown, married, contested, prevailed, acquired accolades, wisdom and multiplied in the diaspora. They have fought with the old conquerors and become one with them. They have returned home bearing exceptional wisdom to tell you we cannot be as we aspire to be, unless we borrow a leaf from those old conquerors. But you look like you know it all. You still prefer to hold on to a system that enslaved you and is still enslaving you into the unknown future.

Formal education only unified known wisdom today. Knowledge is accessible to anyone who have a hand phone and can log into the internet from anywhere on earth. Your refusal to adapt, had intrinsically prevented your use of the vast wisdom available online.

What is a contraption?

Fact one: A contraption like Nigeria cannot depend on its scientists to develop one! ONE crude petroleum refinery. Which schematic data and forms, principles and methods. Resources of hardware and software are clearly obtainable on the internet pages. Of every method of mining and storage, fractionation, refining, processing, safety and controls freely available.

Degrees and scholarships, time and opportunity abound in your local area for which you could call up and recreate exceptional masterpieces for yourselves. But no! We, in the diaspora know that you CANNOT do it because you are still holding up to the age old ancestral norm that failed to help you, that opened you up to slavery and subjugation through several centuries.

We in the diaspora have seen and we are telling you that you must live not exist.

Fact two: In Nigeria, a patient lies on the table and the doctor have two things on his mind: how much is this patient and his/her family paying to carry out this operation. Not as in the diaspora where the doctor tries to redefine the boundaries of health care and maybe make a new breakthrough.

Fact three: A Judge sits in judgement with a gavel in his hands and he looks from the defense to the prosecution, who made the better offer is the question and not the law or the circumstances of facts of the case.

A criminal living in Emirates who called himself Hushpuppi, called an Assistant Inspector general of police (disgraced Nigerian super cop named Abba Kyari) and orders the arrest of his criminal colleague who had suddenly developed cold feet in a criminal transaction. The chief of police only went as far as how many millions was on offer and not on the merits of the false accusation.

The police force is compromised.

The Lecturer returning election results is compromised

Civil servants need oil to sift through files, but your socialization, unknown to you is trickling down to generations yet unborn.

Ihe ojoo gbaa afo oburu Omenala.

So if the peoples, supposedly members of a country, cannot be united under a defined set of goals, ideals, mandate and aspirations be it circular or religious, then they cannot build a national identity. It does not matter whether they are presently laboring under a defined geographical area and suffering under the bondage that is supposed to be a haven for them.

Looking therefore at the implication of this work, nation building had better been left in the hands of the owners of such a nation. But not to arm and allow an invading or occupying neighbor who have acquired military power in whatever way, annihilate the indigenous population. Remember the Universal declaration of human right assures each and every last human being on earth the right to life, right to association, right to self-determination, right for to found a family and the right to unrestrained enjoyment of his or her life unless otherwise as a result of a legal determination following a trial before a competent court. In my next indictment of the UNITED Nation's irresponsibility in the face of the carnage going on in Nigeria, I intend to read out every relevant article of the Universal declaration of Human Rights to point out how these articles have been disregarded by the Buhari's administration in the onslaught against Biafra. I also intend to identify the support being provided to this evil administration by the United Nations, the British government and the government of the United States of America in complete disregard to the provisions of the Universal declaration of Human rights.

Thank you for listening, my name is Iwunna.

Our Destination is Biafra

"Where are you going to?" A question we hear thrown at us by people we meet along the way. Our words in answer may portray an inherent intent yes, but, it is our actions that determine whether we reach the destination, we say we intend to achieve.

There is this practice world leaders have adopted known as the "State of the Nation address." In many nations of the world, this ritual is an annual event when the President or the Prime Minister takes the center stage in more ways than one. He or She goes to a joint session of both houses of parliament to deliver a speech. In this speech, the leader presents his report card, which at the time in point shows how the country is performing under his or her stewardship.

The Leader in the state of the nation address is expected to outline how he/she had piloted the affairs of the nation for that year or through a defined period. This speech includes every important aspect of National life that had need of attention, what was done and is being done to make national life a success for all citizens. It includes administration, economy, education, health, commerce and industry, foreign affairs security and others. This address does not have a question and answer session so the leader is not burdened with thinking of how to face the media. He only presents to his people, his policies and what had been done or will be done to alleviate their problems and carry them along in his administration, in the short-run.

Well I believe we are overdue for a state of the nation address. Buhari has completed a first term in office and is halfway into his second term in office.

In all these years, many reports have been made, projected and circulated both from local and international press, of the work of international organizations or state departments. A lot have happened too and there is need for Buhari to present a report card to Nigeria.

I will draw from those records and historical data to present to us all, the state of the Nation under President Muhamadu Buhari. This my report will also rely on data produced by this very administration, then we will call up data from two former administrations of Eastern regions in other to understand the state of the nation at present.

The National Bureau of statistics reported that between January 2016 and 30th September 2017, 8 million people lost their jobs in Nigeria.

Between 2015 and May 2017, youth unemployment climbed from 13.7% to 33.1% and from 40.8% in January 2020 to 53.4% by January 2021. This means that out of 100 youths who are able and ready to work regardless of the skills they possess, 54 of them cannot have a job presently.

Inflation rate stood at 18.12% in April 2021.

We know that popular global economic reviews almost always stop at the contribution of crude oil and Natural gas into the Nigeria's economy. What we may not know is that, this is a calculated denial by the government and international economic bodies to discuss, acknowledge or encourage attention to the other sectors of Nigerian economy by the Nigerian populace. I mean there is a clear conspiracy between the governing clique and international bodies that do business with Nigeria, this had been ongoing before 1960's. Once economic details states: 80% to 95% of Nigerian international earner is oil, there is an automatic discount of other sectors into a broad category as 'others' giving the idea that their contributions are negligible or not important to be mentioned at all.

In the solid mineral industry some minerals that are being mined in Nigeria includes Gold, Lead oxide, Iron ore and about 44 other natural mineral occurrences. A number of these minerals, including Nickel, Bitumen, Iron Ore and Coal are estimated to exist in commercial quantities, meanwhile there is a 53.4 % unemployment rate in the country presently.

In the area of tourism; this nation have vast and rich cultural heritage which should had been strategically repositioned to partner tourism as its driver to lift the Nigerian economy. Harvest festivals, fishing festivals, cultural sites, carnivals, museums, interesting archeological sites and natural wonders. Development of rivers as transport waterways, ocean cruise tours, hotels, forest trails, arts and crafts. Important sporting events could be commissioned into helping to provide much needed boost to the economy, create employment for the teeming youths of this country. Instead, Buhari's administration brought in terrorists, bandits, killer herdsmen, guns and started promoting the displacement of indigenous people.

From Agriculture, Nigeria is a powerhouse for food production and cash crops production. Food crops like cassava, tomatoes, onions, cucumber, yams, plantain and banana, maize, rice and other grains. Cash crops like cashew, groundnuts, Cocoa, oil palm, cotton, Jute among others. We are a major food production nation in West Africa. But when you have used bandits and herdsmen to destroy farms and the farming communities. When you have committed your farming communities to Internally Displaced People (IDP) camps, where would the food for the nation come from, before we talk of exports.

Education/Health: Our youths now go to Ghana for education especially those who had not been marked for assasination by the Nigerian security outfits. The health sector is comatose. As far as Buhari is concerned, as President of Nigeria, this nation could as well die because he considers that the Fulani are not talented enough to engage in almost all sectors of the economy except looting, banditry, terrorism and cattle rearing. So those are the only sectors of the economy, he is interested in. I mean looting, banditry, terrorism, cattle herding, lies and corruption. Under Buhari, Fulani must be aided to kill, rape, burn and displace all other indigenous groups. Under Buhari, they must be left in peace to practice their kidnapping for ransom trade, allowed to pillage farms, lead their cows wherever it pleases them without questions, take over indigenous villages and towns, summarily execute them, take over their houses and communities rename these villages and so on.

The Chandler Good Government Index (CGGI), ranks countries according to government capabilities and effectiveness. Out of the 104 countries surveyed, Nigeria ranked 102. Only Zimbabwe and Venezuela performed worse. Nigeria is the third worst nation in the world! Imagine that? The aspects used for this analysis are 1) leadership and foresight; 2) robust laws and policies; 3) strong institutions; 4) financial stewardship; 6) attractive marketplace; 7) global influence and reputation; and 8) helping people rise out of poverty.

United Nations Human Development Index, (UNHDI) for 2020 puts Nigeria at 168th position out of 173 countries. The World Bank ranked Nigeria the 6th worst country in its 2020 Human Capital Index. Human capital index refers to amount of human capital that 'a child born today' can expect to attain by age 18, given the risks of poor health and poor education that prevail in the country where he or she lives. In other words, the question asks: **what are the chances that a child born in Nigeria today can grow up to acquire needed skills to benefit his/her country in eighteen years from today**? Human Capital Index is measured from present circumstances at the time of analysis. The result of UN HDI presently says that a child born in Nigeria today has **a zero** chance of successful growth, health, education and training to attain her potential and become useful to Nigeria. For your information, Niger is ranked 173 out of 173 so Buhari is dragging us down to join Niger, Chad 172, Mali 171, and South Sudan 170 as the worst nations that have no plans for their future.

I will now present to you from historical data, the stewardship of Mazi Michael Iheonukara Okpara. I am doing this to show, the value which you and I place on people we consider as our leaders, not all of them are leaders. Through time, these leaders had been influenced and compromised by the situation of Nigeria. Nigeria as an entity, is an evil rot, a virus which infects and destroys the mind of all those who have poor principles and integrity. Therefore, we must be able to make a choice and accept leaders who cannot be bought or compromised by any inducements either from western nations or from perks available as a result of their political position of power.

Mazi Iheonukara Okpara was the Premier of Eastern region from 1959 to 1966. Wikipedia documented that "at 39, he was the nation's youngest Premier. He was a strong advocate of what he called "pragmatic socialism" and believed that agricultural reform was crucial to the ultimate success of Nigeria. He set for himself a mission to help, improve, develop and justify the trust his people placed in him when he was elected into power. Let us see some of his records of accomplishment in the four years six months, he was in power.

For sheer expediency because his records of accomplishment are not in dispute I shall list some of these institutions established by M.I. Okpara when he was the premier and Francis Akanu Ibiam was the Governor of eastern region. Okpara established the Eastern Nigerian development Corporation as a vessel to carry out his vision of economic transformation of eastern Nigeria. They embarked on rapid development of the region into becoming the fastest developing region in the world in the I960's.

1) 1962 to 1968: Farm settlements were established across eastern region. There were two types of farm settlements he established a) cash crop estates, which incorporated processing centers in preparation for the export market and b) Food crops farm settlement for local food crops production.

These settlements are listed as:

Ulonnam – Umuahia, Ohaji- Uguta, Igbariam-Onitsha, Boki – Ogoja, Uzouwani,-Enugu, Abak,- Annang, each of these farm settlements were to accommodate 5000 farmers who were expected to gain self-sufficiency in 5 years of the project. Today Malaysian farm settlements under the Federal land development Authority (FELDA) is responsible for palm oil, rubber production and other cash and food crops across the nation which feeds the nation and have placed Malaysia at the top in the production of the palm oil and rubber in the world for decades. Incidentally, the Malaysian system modeled after the Eastern Nigerian system, had actually received technical assistance and seed setts from National Institute for Oil Palm Research NIFOR Benin.

So what happened? Nigeria happened to those Eastern Region farm settlements.

2) Michelin Factory for tyre production Port Harcourt

3) Universal Insurance Company with operations across the nation

4) Nigerian Gas Factory Emene Enugu

5) Aluminum Factory Port Harcourt
6) Glass factory Port Harcourt
7) Asbestos Cement Factory Emene Enugu
8) Central bank Port Harcourt
9) Golden Guinea breweries Umuahia
10) Presidential Hotel Port Harcourt
11) Nkalagu Cement factory
12) Modern ceramics Industries Umuahia
13) Textile mills Aba
14) Textile mills Onitsha
15) Shoe factory Owerri
16) University of Nigeria Nsukka

In other to do achieve these, it is recorded that Okpara delegated the day to day running of the then political party to Dr L. C. Mbanugo, civil service to Sam Oti, intelligentsia to Professor Kalu Ezera and economy to Mazi Odumegwu Ojukwu Snr. Thus creating a mini-cabinet as it were beyond the formal structures of the party and administrative bureaucracy. He directly exercised an inspiring overview to the business of governance through formal structures of governance. He did these because he wanted his work in uplifting the region to be achieved. He wanted to create jobs for the new leaders and educated class and the entire population of the eastern region. He spread those establishments around the entire region without any trace of nepotism and cronyism because he believed every citizen of the region is equally entitled to every available opportunities. M.I. Okpara was a true statesman, he lived up to his responsibilities as a premier.

Chief Samuel Onunaka Mbakwe; (De Sam, as he was fondly called), was sworn in as Governor of Imo State on Monday 1st October, 1979. It was a four-year tenure. Imo State territory De Sam Mbakwe governed included present Imo State, Abia State and Afikpo geographical areas of Ebonyi State, known as Ebonyi-South

Senatorial District. It was, indeed, a very large State. The main challenge he faced was to redevelop a territory that had been ravaged by the Nigerian/Biafran civil war.

Remember that this was at a time when the impoverishment policy of seizing all monies owned by Igbos in exchange for 20 Naira was still hurting the people. There were several other policies Igbos would only become aware of as time went on especially with respect to glass ceilings, enhanced quota which totally discriminated against Igbos. Governor did not let any of those problems distract him, De Sam Mbakwe started with aggressive road infrastructure in Aba, Owerri, Umuahia, Okigwe, Afikpo and to Asa Local Government Area, which he had created. He linked all these towns together with an excellent road network.

Mbakwe then turned his attention to Agriculture, Education, Tourism, Aviation and Industrialization of the state.

He established two gigantic farms: Imo Modern Poultry Farm, Avutu in Obowo and Ogwe Golden Chicken project in Asa.

He established Imo state university, designed to be a multi-campus University, with each Senatorial district hosting a major College or faculty of the University.

He built a five Star Hotel, Concord Hotel in Owerri. It was the best Hotel, East of the Niger.

Enyimba Hotel at Aba was still under construction at the time of Buhari's coup d'etat.

He built an Airport at Owerri, known today as Sam Mbakwe Airport. Till today Sam Mbakwe airport is the only airport built with financial contributions by the people of the state in Nigeria.

On industrialization, Mbakwe established Aluminium Smelter Plant in Inyishi.

A Paint Factory at Aboh Mbaise.

A Power Plant at Amaraku.

All this time Samuel Onunaka Mbakwe had continued to maintain and support all the existing companies set up by Dr. M.I. Ọkpara, before the war.

Mbakwe like Ọkpara spread development schemes and projects equally into all areas of the state he governed. This method of development was not an abberation at all, for Igbo culture seeks the involvement of every member of its society in the activities of the society right from decision making to carrying out those decisions and in the enjoyment of dividends therefrom. Traditional Igbo societies viewed all its members as equal.

In fact, the rot which over took Nigeria (even though then as undertones since everyone initially worked to make Nigeria a success), set in when Muhammadu Buhari unceremoniously toppled the elected government of Shehu Shagari. Like he is doing now 2015 to 2023, Buhari brought the nation down to its knees with his wickedness and evil mind, so much that his lieutenants toppled his government due to what they perceived as a total disregard to law and order by then General Muhamadu Buhari.

It was the prolonged period of military rule, when the soldiers used the academia to device policies for which they had no intentions of carrying through. When they used experts to milk the country dry, setting in place a culture of might over thought. Money in exchange for ready-made designs, schemes in exchange for truth, that the bastardization of Nigeria took on national colors.

The military is an organization built on a culture of 'might is right'. Only the administrative cadres of military institutions delve into organization and strategy still this aspect, only in terms of achieving the ultimate goal to subdue and conquer. Soldiers are not meant, taught or prepared for civil society engagement; they are not conditioned for to engage their own people with time or patience. We must realize that the army cannot understand the world as you see it. Now when you have this, in an embodiment of ethnic myopic tendencies of Buhari spanning decades, Nigeria was a keg of gunpowder ready to explode and it has.

A popular adage says, whomever you surround yourself with, informs who you are. When we listen to leaders who have no answers to our problems, that is all we get: **NO ANSWERS TO OUR PROBLEMS**. There is the assertion that through these long period of bad leadership, Nigeria have developed an age of people taught and socialized in the language of irresponsibility, which had been translated into unfeeling, irresponsible and corrupt class of people amongst us leading a people who respond only to excitement of their eyes and not their minds.

Assuming I wish to go to the stream to fetch water, and I pick up my bucket or water-can and embark on my journey. I walk from my house to the village square and turn left towards the market square. I spent ten minutes walking to the market. My friend Chukas asks me “ de Okechukwu where are you going?” and I reply “I am going to the stream to fetch water.” After spending thirty minutes chatting with him, I leave and start in the direction of the forest still holding my empty water container. On the way I meet another friend, Amaka, she is returning from the farms carrying a load of firewood on her head, we chat for a while and I tell her that I need to keep going, since I was going to the stream to fetch some water. Then I continue on the journey. I pass through three farm fields and come out to Isiala Ngwa. All this while, I have been telling everyone who cares to listen, that I am on an errand to fetch water for my use. Yet the roads I had taken, will never lead me to any streams in our village or any river, or water bodies whatsoever. I have travelled far through four villages along the way and I am still holding my empty water container with me.

Nigerians are all carrying empty water cans, we are telling the world that we are on a journey to fetch water we need for our use, but we are carefully, intentionally, making sure in every way, that we WILL NEVER pass through any streams or water bodies on our endless self-defeating journey. We will never amount to anything unless we take the only road through which we will move definitely to a set purpose in life, to our own nation states.

Save Biafran Souls Group

Biafran in Diaspora,
Melaka Malaysia
4th June, 2021.

The Prosecutor,
Information and Evidence Unit,
Office of the Prosecutor,
Post Office Box 19519,
2500CM The Hague,
The Netherlands.

Dear Sir/Madam,

APPEAL AND SUBMISSION OF EVIDENCES FOR A DETERMINATION OF THE EXISTENCE OF POSSIBLE ON-GOING GENOCIDE AGAINST INDIGENOUS PEOPLE IN NIGERIA

Introduction

Why do we have the power of thought, or memory, the power of recall and the ability to put life in perspective, which other lower life forms do not have. Creation had gifted man the wisdom to husband the earth, to subdue the earth and to make a paradise for life on earth. Religion assures us that the other place where life exits is in the world where we can never go with this physical body; Heaven or hell, Nirvana, Paradise or whatever it is called in various religions, the thought is still the same even to those that profess no faith at all. Igbo native religion refers to it as the land of our 'fore-fathers'. To enter it, we must be found worthy of a meaningful life here on earth before we are admitted there, after death. Science has tried, is trying still to find another planet in the myriads of stars across the limitless space. Until such a life is physically found, or until another planet is able to supply earth-like characteristics, granting us another home, we have no other home than planet EARTH. That means that we have a duty to husband this earth for the benefit of mankind. Human thought, wisdom and convictions are more diverse than the diversity of our clear racial divide of colors: black at one extreme and white to the other extreme.

In 1966, a group of army officers launched a coup d'etat in Nigeria. The country Nigeria, thereafter selected an ethnic group for extermination. When the ethnicities involved, tried to protect itself, Nigerian nation fought with the help of then world super powers: United Kingdom, Russia and their Egypt and Arab allies to annihilate the Biafrans. I would not talk about how wars help weapon producing nations to sell their weapons and make money on the back of oceans and rivers of blood; we know that the super powers are the weapon producing nations then and now. **This document is an appeal for deliverance from an ongoing genocide because, for all instances and purposes the 1966 -1970 war has not ended.** This document is an update on other documents that had been sent to you previously (2017, 2020).

Genocide as a word has a recent history. In determination of the age of the world, anything less than a thousand years is young, though it is interesting that what constitutes an age also is affected by the standard of persons or people who consider themselves world's opinion creators or the conscience of the world. There was a time when most of the world gave preference to Europe to lead and to forge a pathway for the world. What a good work they did, if we may say so. Two world wars, colonial wars that decimated ninety percent of the new world's population. It was all a bid to wipe out every other race and ethnic identities and take over ancient cultures and natural resources. We should have a name for it even just for establishing a historical context alone: 'ntondu'. The word "nto" is from Igbo meaning "to steal" or "to kidnap"; "ndu" is also Igbo word for "life". NTONDU therefore means to take away, replace or subjugate life for the purposes of the aggressor. Ntondu was the basic gifts the new worlds received during colonialization ntondu from United Kingdom, Germany, France, Spain, Portugal, Belgium, Indonesia, Sudan, Nigeria, Cameroun, Brazil etc. It spread with the independence. Igbo si na: "Ife ojoo gba afo oburu Omenala" (If evil continues for a long time it becomes a tradition).

Across the board colonial masters carried out ntondu at every new lands they visited, from Australia to South Africa, from India to Alaska, from Peru to Timor Timur. Yet as independence was gained, ethnicities jostled for supremacy against each other. Ntondu now took the shade of who was more desperate, who had more weapons, who was seriously determined to carry it out without flinching at the sight of rivers of blood. The colonialist in many instances just wanted to get out with their loot, so whoever offered to take the mantle of authority, whoever offered to control the administration of these colonies was welcome to take over without a thought to it. This may be legally wrong as the colonial masters having disrupted the natural order of hitherto independent nations could not let just them all go back to the wars of ancient 'hunter/gatherer' periods like that. Nevertheless, that was what they did, when they coalesced large areas like Sudan into one nation. Nigeria became a single nation with over 100 different languages, more than 50 distinct nations all completely different in every way: culture, language, dressing, way of life, religion, aspirations and physical features even. The nomadic Fulani herdsmen and the sedentary Hausa farmers, the royal kingdoms of Bini and other Yoruba nations. With village/town based Igbo clans where a village council (made up of family elders) independently govern their villages from time immemorial, (the first known democratic system anywhere on earth). Thanks to colonialism and the 1914 amalgamation, they all must forge a single entity together with all other nations caught up in the vast area designated as Nigeria.

Genocide as a word therefore have a recent history because all those other killings done at the times we attribute as past were not codified, or were accepted as the tradition of those times.

How recent is recent or how far into the past is past. They that codified the necessary laws did so, preserving for themselves, a special position which absolved them from responsibilities for crimes clearly committed with the basic intention required for legal liability, However 'he' who wrote the law could not be held accountable for crimes committed before the laws came into force. They were free from ntondu committed against all natural laws of man.

In the light of the steady killings being perpetrated in Nigeria against the Indigenous People Of Biafra (IPOB) and against Christians. There have been repeated calls from inside and outside Nigeria. By members of Nigerian religious organizations, churches, Nigerian parliamentarians and Governors of states so affected. Calls by International bodies too and we know such must be present in dispatches of responsible ambassadorial reports sent to their governments. Nigerian situation is clear to the entire world. The government of Biafra in exile has been doing everything it can to get International attention. Yours truly have also written a concise letter attaching pictorial evidence to the Under-secretary of the United Nations offices in Geneva, yet the calls of a declaration that there is possible genocide being perpetrated by Buhari's government by proxies and by direct police and military forces has seemingly not been heeded by the United Nations.

We would desist from joining allegations that Nigeria is buying the ambassadors of nations or lobbying powerful nations to look the other way. It is entirely hypocritical for that Nigerian lady Amina, to sit at the UN and receive a report presented by the brother of George Floyd who was killed by a US police officer, when Nigeria is killing its citizens with complete abandon and no one seems accountable to these killings. Yes, there are reports showing that United State is watching the Nigerian situation, but then we consider it too little in the circumstances. The silence of the international community is a tacit support that the killings can go on. Mind you in case someone would tomorrow suggest that IPOB and the voices were not clear enough:

Our Allegations (internet links to pictorial/video evidence included)

1. We allege that President Muhamadu Buhari is using the Nigerian police, the Nigerian civil defense forces and the Nigerian armed forces to kill Christians, ethnic Igbos, and other indigenous peoples of the country; and they are doing so without any let up, without any reason whatsoever. The security forces barge into homes, university hostels, markets, streets, churches and offices, they abduct ethnic Igbos kill them on the spot or take them away and these people are never seen again.

2. We allege that there is systematic ethnic cleansing, where in Fulani militia disguised as Herdsmen are killing everyone in middle beltern villages in Nigeria. They target, they arrive, they kill everyone save the escapees, and they rename the villages and take over the homes, farms, and towns of 'cleared' villages.

3. We allege that Boko Haram terrorists aligned with the Islamic State West Africa have stepped up attacks and taken over a large land mass in Nigeria with the tacit support of Buhari's government.

4. We allege that Christians in Southern Kaduna are on the verge of TOTAL annihilation and the state and federal government has no answer to these
killings.

5. We allege also that to enhance these annihilation, the government of Kaduna have steadily arrested local youths trying to protect themselves and their homes leaving their women and elderly exposed to killings yet no Bandits, herdsmen or anyone has ever been arrested for killings that count into hundreds each time these Fulani killers attack.

6. We allege that our women and girls are being raped and murdered systematically, probably as scare tactics.

7. We allege that farms are being destroyed intentionally, farmers chased out of their land and homes at gun point, women and girls abducted and taken away most not to be seen again.

8. We allege that the police and army at the orders of the President of Nigeria are murdering Igbos and other ethnic groups of southern Nigeria, at the
slightest excuse.

9. We allege that many of these atrocities are all being filmed and circulated online by the perpetrators in which case the question arises, why no one especially the United Nations have attempted to raise some eye brows.
So we went to check the United Nations documents on genocide.

The Wikipedia has a few definitions:

Genocide [ˈdʒɛnəsʌɪd]

NOUN: the deliberate killing of a large group of people, especially those of a particular nation or ethnic group. "a campaign of genocide" · [more] synonyms:
racial killing · massacre · wholesale slaughter · mass slaughter · wholesale killing · indiscriminate killing · mass murder · mass homicide · mass
destruction · annihilation · extermination · elimination · liquidation · eradicati on · decimation · butchery · bloodbath · bloodletting · pogrom · ethnic cleansing · holocaust · Shoah · slaying · battue · hecatomb genocide (n.)
The word was actually formed by Polish-born U.S. jurist Raphael Lemkin
(1900-1959) "killing a tribe," it combined two greek words: 'genos' meaning 'race' -cide "a killing." (That should be enough of the definition for now).
But there has been instances that have plagued humanity over the centuries which were termed populicide (1799), from French populicide, of 1792, a word from the Revolution, which was turned to English in 1893 as folk-murdering.

Going by the United Nations convention therefore, we would assume that genocide means the intentional action to kill off a people entirely (usually defined as an ethnic, national, racial, or religious group) it does not matter whether the action is entirely successful or not, in so far as there was an intention and the action to produce the desired result.

According to the United Nations Convention on the Prevention and Punishment of the Crime of Genocide (UNCPPCG) Article 2.78 **there are five main aspects that must be proven for a determination of genocide to be made**:

1) **Killing members of the group**: The act does not enquire that the entire group be annihilated before genocide could be determined. Therefore, we ask the United Nations, please send in one of her officials to take up residence in any part of Nigeria, please bring a chair, paper and pen to continue counting with us. It is apparent that these several hundred thousand over the years are not yet enough for you. Or maybe you assume we are burying empty boxes by the thousands every week. Come and join us please send a representative to burry some of the boxes with us. This August week is ok? Come along, the Fulani has not finished with us yet.

2) **Causing serious bodily or mental harm to members of the group**: There are those torture method devised by the Army and presently in use in southern Nigeria. The first is to tie up the IPOB with their hands behind their backs and tie the legs similarly then arch the victim backwards, the victim is then hung on those ropes onto the rafters of the roof and a fireplace is started under him. There is the second method of making their victims swim in and drink sewage or open drainage ponds. Flogging, beatings and anything that comes to their minds. Just open Facebook, these are entirely in the public domain. Filmed and posted by the men who are carrying out these atrocities.

3) **Deliberately inflicting on the group conditions of life calculated to bring about its physical destruction in whole or in part**: Nigeria has maintained a quota system through which Biafran progress is stifled. Stated as EDUCATIONALLY DISADVANTAGED. The Fulani and Hausa ethnic groups are the only race or ethnic group in the world who have branded themselves as being of a low mental capability and therefore must be accepted at as low as 3% passing scale to qualify for College admission. Whereas the Igbos and Biafrans and Yorubas must attain 70% to gain entrance to the same school, college or university in Nigeria. This is a complete lie and a disservice to itself. It demeans its human quality and is entirely responsible to the inability of the Fulani/Hausa races to hitherto attempt to compete fairly with other Nigerian ethnicities, had created mistrust and enmity and skewered meritocracy in Nigeria. Quotas are similarly placed in everything this has stifled academic and professional development,

Had affected the quality of manpower and is seen at every facet of national life.
International relations are undertaken by officers who are not qualified but were appointed because of quota system.
Contract negotiations were almost always signed at the detriment of national interests because Nigerian negotiators are quota appointed whereas the country boasts the best level of experts in all fields of endeavor.
Infrastructural development must be approved based on which region is allowed to develop or not. Today there are no good roads, No operational seaports and No international airports in Biafraland, though it holds one of the largest oil reserve in Africa, Nigeria does not have a serviceable refinery, the country have to engage in deals that cost it the value of its natural wealth in other to export crude and 're-import' refined oil. We are ashamed, because local institutions, infrastructure and human skills and knowledge that

would have been created and developed by concerted effort in the oil industry mining /refining /education/jobs /tourism) are lost.
Military checkpoints are placed at one kilometer distance all over Eastern Nigerian roads whereas the war against Boko Haram and other terrorist organizations are in the Northeast and North central of Nigeria. These infringes on the third Article II(b)of the Genocide convention, amounting to torture, cruel, inhuman, degrading treatment and punishment and all are being committed with the requisite intention to destroy ethnic Igbos and Biafrans and Christians in Nigeria.
A few examples of known genocides carried out in the world are the Holocaust by Nazi Germany against Jews, the Armenian Genocide, the Native American genocide, the Cambodian genocide, and the Bosnian genocide, the Anfal genocide, the Darfur genocide, the Rwandan genocide. Wikipedia list of world known genocides included the Biafran genocide. "(1966 Nigerian counter-coup during which Johnson Aguiyi-Ironsi and Yakubu Gowon seized power leading to a series of massacres against the Igbo tribe. These massacres were hypothesized to have been organized beforehand,[367] Nigerian leadership later began to intentionally promote the extermination of the Igbo. The slaughter lead to the deaths of 8,000 to 30,000 Igbo men, women, and children, resulting in the secession of Eastern Nigeria into the State of Biafra.)" (1. 2.)

According to the texts of the UNHCR [7] "genocide does not necessarily mean the immediate destruction of a nation, except when accomplished by mass killings of all members of a nation. It is intended rather to signify a coordinated plan of different actions aiming at the destruction of essential foundations of the life of national groups, with the aim of annihilating the groups themselves."
We begin to wonder if the meaning we get from reading the above quoted text is exactly same as the United Nation Organization does.

Especially when the document tried to push the narrative that a determination of the existence of a genocide whether in the past or presently ongoing is a matter for academic exercise. The basic truth is that when there is an intention to wipe out entirely or in part an ethnic group, and action carried out to achieve this purpose, genocide is determined to have been or is being committed. This is as simple as A, B, C. It is for the courts to make a ruling that such is the case in point. Why do we need to wait until half of the targeted group is killed off, before we need to take action? Watch it carefully! The times have drastically changed and the present crop of world leadership should be an indication of what is in store for the world in the present and nearest future. There was a time a single 15 cm hair-comb or let me use a better item, a Lady's facial-mirror would buy a sixteen year old British boy an entire town in Africa. Go and try it today! It was just about five years ago that someone who did not have what it takes to be a leader of the greatest nation on earth won an election on the basic truth (without its attendant finesse) of the dangers the world faced. Then everyone was toying with political correctness while he declared he wanted to MAKE AMERICA GREAT AGAIN; today we can appreciate how difficult the United State is finding it for having allowed the great lie in the first place. There is no safe haven for anyone again. Afghanistan created a generation of terrorists because the world allowed the problem to fester from a Russian invasion. It is still ongoing thirty years on, have spawn greater evils around the world: Syria, Iraq, Yemen and the genocide against Yazidis. You can argue that all these are discrete. I disagree because evil will always seeks a homeland. These terrorists need a safe haven from where to operate. Instability offers them that opportunity, but they come with their traditional hallmark of death and destruction. ISWAP is now in Nigeria. The case of the Islamic uprising in the north east of Nigeria started with a disgruntled colleague in a power tussle and metamorphosed to Boko Haram. Now it has given the leeway to

ISWAP and has been drawn into an age-old hatred of the Igboman's skills and propensity to success. In Buhari the world saw a proxy leader, the type Britain wishes to have to keep Nigeria where it belongs: UNDER THE TABLE. We bet they did not wish for a genocide, but it was there all the while. He said it. There was the Boko Haram threat in existence. They chose him to be their Spokesman. He even demanded that the terrorists MUST NOT BE ATTACKED. In the meantime, he had declared: "DO EVERYTHING IN MY POWER AT ALL TIMES TO ENSURE THE COMPLETE AND TOTAL IMPLEMENTATION OF SHARIA IN NIGERIA!" So what was it we did not know? Nigeria is 55% Christians; tell me how you can impose Sharia in 100% of the country?

The United Nations General Assembly adopted the Convention on the Prevention and Punishment of the Crime of Genocide (CPPCG) in 1948 and furthermore declared that the "denial of the right of existence of entire human groups, shocks the conscience of mankind, results in great losses to humanity in the form of cultural and other contributions represented by these human groups, and is contrary to moral law and the spirit and aims of the United Nations" (22), so enforce the law.

Reckless Use Of Politics Against Good Judgement

The issue of acceptance of all members of the United Nations to the genocide convention would give us an insight to the workings of the world Body. The USSR then was opposed to the convention as it feared it may be caught in the webs of the convention because of its treatment of the many nations under the USSR 23.25 Other nations similarly sought to limit effectiveness of the conventions when it comes to killings they termed 'political'. African proverb say: "when crocodiles eat their young, what will they not do to the skin of a Lizard?" what will Britain not do to Igbo people if they did not care for United Nations sanctions against them and a looming Gulf war in weaponizing Saddam Hussein against the world. It is high time the world should call for self-determination for Biafra. It has been more than 60 years following the Civil war yet Biafra had not stopped clamoring for self-determination. We purposely would not delve into the issues of mens rea or actus rea in talking about Genocide against Biafra and Christians in Nigeria. A fact that has always been there right from Colonial times. Firstly, because I am not a lawyer, secondly I am so incensed with the behavior of the world to rationally control myself not to call you all manner of names and or curse you and all your generations inclusive. If Britain is honest to itself, of course it cannot (UK sold equipment for weapons of war to Iraq, when its own soldiers amongst other nations, were preparing to go to war against Iraq). Is there any more reprehensive behavior you can ever think of in the history of the world? We challenge you to mention it here. Search online for: Iraq affair "Arms for Iraq: scandal hits fan". The Economist. 325: 64. 1 January 1992. ISSN 0013-0613.).

Of course Britain and Russia together with Nigeria fought Biafra in the 1966-70 war too. The United Nation should please ask United Kingdom what Biafrans did wrong to them. Another reality, maybe, the world is trying to push their narrow sectarian view in the Biafran case. There is marked exclusion of social and political entities as targets of genocide in the genocide document as interpreted by experts of the UN Charter. M. Hassan Kakar, had said that the international definition of genocide is too restricted [66], that it should include political groups or any group so defined by the perpetrator.

"Genocide is a form of one-sided mass killing in which a state or other authority intends to destroy a group, that group and membership of it, defined by the perpetrator," Chalk and Jonassohn.

Nigeria this age, must be seen for what it is. Attempts to turn a blind eye to the injustices of Nigeria by the international community must be called out for what it is. We all know the reason why many, especially among the ruling class, are seemingly content to let things remain as they are irrespective of the collapse of common sense and wisdom; a tacit understanding that **if you tow the line of the leader no matter how irresponsible they are** you are safe. That is untrue. Leadership by duress is terrorism in itself no matter how the party or the leader entered the seat of government.

The concept of 'government' incorporates the surrender of collective autonomy of the citizens of a nation, in exchange for consideration of the common good of all, in terms of every activities and pronouncements of the government. In the institution of democratic government no single individual or a specified group within such a nation is/are anticipated would be or remain the leader(s) of a given nation certainly not in Nigeria. There is a social contract theory, which establishes a moral and political rules of behavior in every society on earth. We must know the relative ambits of social contract under a constitution is guided by morality of common law. You cannot force me to trace the works of men like Socrates, Thomas Hobbes, John Locke, Jean Jacques Ronsseau and so many others, in other to condition your mind to the basic demands of a job you applied and campaigned for. A job you claimed you have the qualifications for and which somehow you achieved by hook or crook. The reason for structured formal and informal education in a nation is systematic preparation of the conduct of every citizen of the nation for the roles they must play in their lives towards a society that deliver common good, harmony, peace and justice for all when they attain certain standards with time.

Traditional Biafran thoughts and wisdom is a republican outlook: **Onye biri ibe ya biri. Biri kam biri. Egbe bere ugo bere. Onweghi onye bu Nnam oha.**

Muhammadu Buhari
@MBuhari

Many of those misbehaving today are too young to be aware of the destruction and loss of lives that occurred during the Nigerian Civil War. Those of us in the fields for 30 months, who went through the war, will treat them in the language they understand.

Plates

https://www.anaedoonline.ng/2021/06/02/latest-president-buhari-threatensigbos-with-second-civil-war/

NEWS

Fulani will rule forever, we are flagging off security outfit across Nigeria – Miyetti Allah

Published 11 seconds agoon June 6, 2020
By **John Owen Nwachukwu**

FG orders forensic audit of Discos

FG makes a U-turn, admits B'Haram targeting Christians

S'West Assemblies to pass Amotekun bill on Tuesday

How Saraki diverted Kwara N1obn – EFCC

The PUNCH

21 killed as police, vigilantes battle Katsina bandits
Page 41

Bauchi gov heads PDP panel probing 2019 elections

FRIDAY, FEBRUARY 28, 2020

N200

Repentant terrorists to enjoy foreign education – Senate bill

Pages 2 & 41

- UBEC, TETFund to fund rehabilitated insurgents' agency
- Buhari called seven months after Leah Sharibu's abduction – Mother

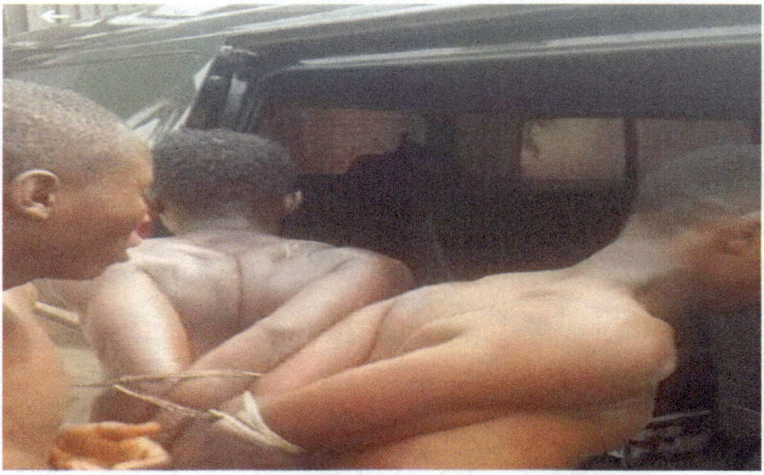

Micheal Ejiofor
24 Sep 2019 at 4:13 am •

TIME FOR JUSTICE HAS COME....

We wish to appeal to all Biafrans in Biafra land who have suffered any sort of torture, harm, or lost any of his relation in the hands of the Nigeria security apparatus since (2015) during all our manifestation, to please come forward for the time for justice has come.

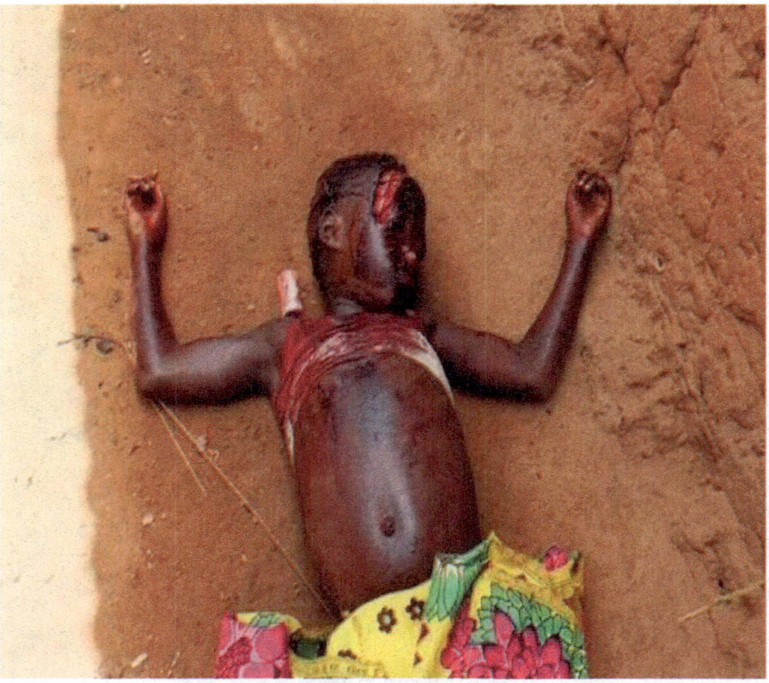

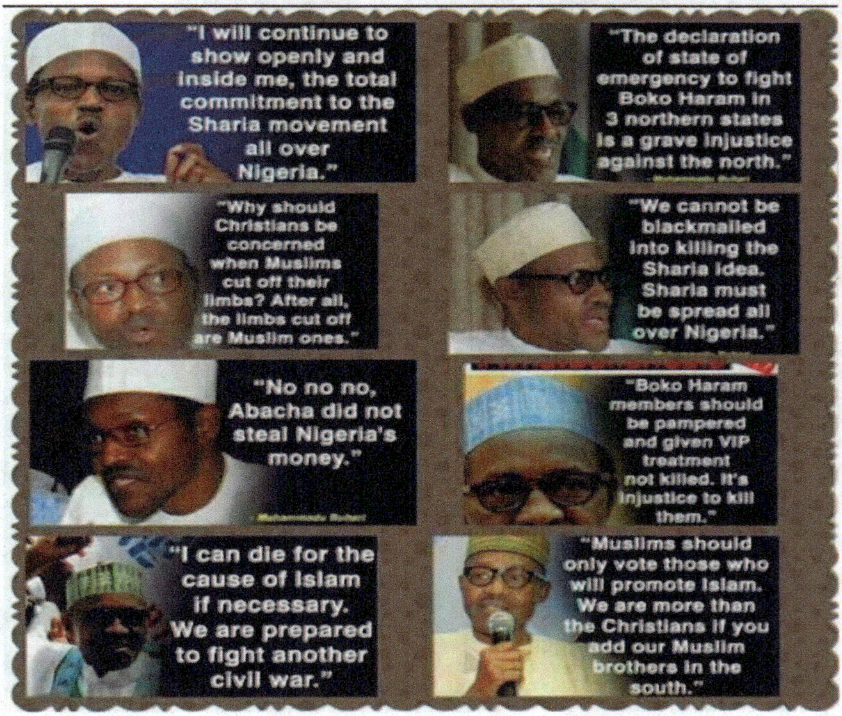
"I will continue to show openly and inside me, the total commitment to the Sharia movement all over Nigeria."
"The declaration of state of emergency to fight Boko Haram in 3 northern states is a grave injustice against the north."
"Why should Christians be concerned when Muslims cut off their limbs? After all, the limbs cut off are Muslim ones."
"We cannot be blackmailed into killing the Sharia idea. Sharia must be spread all over Nigeria."
"No no no, Abacha did not steal Nigeria's money."
"Boko Haram members should be pampered and given VIP treatment not killed. It's injustice to kill them."
"I can die for the cause of Islam if necessary. We are prepared to fight another civil war."
"Muslims should only vote those who will promote Islam. We are more than the Christians if you add our Muslim brothers in the south."

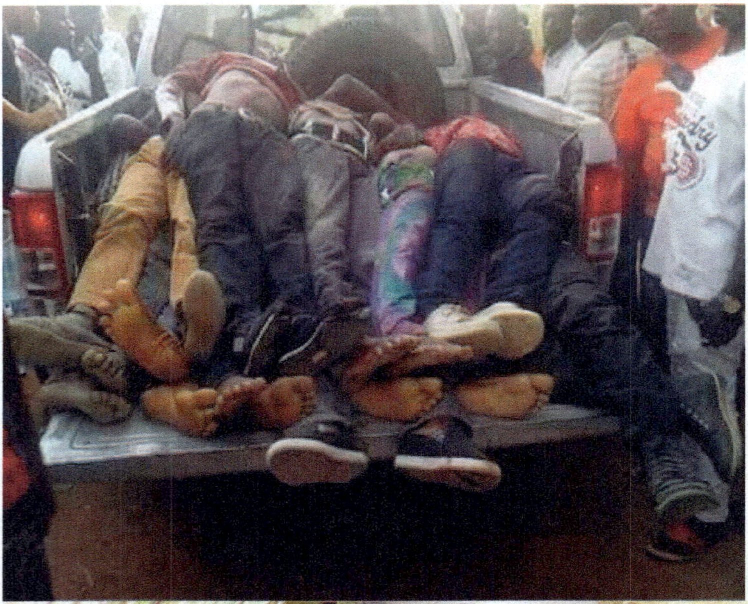

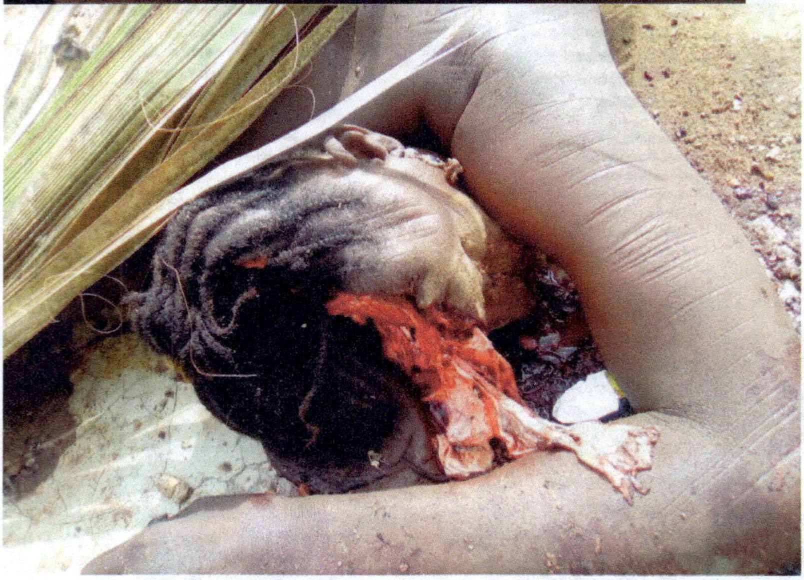

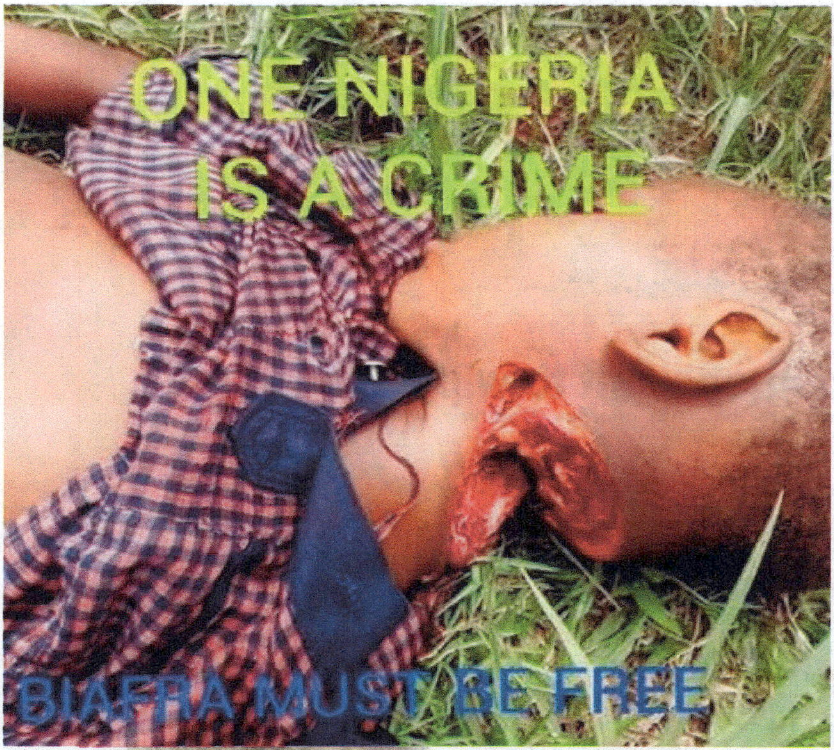
ONE NIGERIA
IS A CRIME
BIAFRA MUST BE FREE

A Publication of the Catholic Diocese of Ahiara, Mbaise, Imo State, Nigeria

THE GUIDE

In Truth To Peace

Vol. 22. No. 16, June 7 2020. ISSN 1116-1663 ₦100

Nnamdi Kanu is blackmailing me in order to be incharge of Biafra struggle - Uwazuruke

Left to right - Most. Rev. Moses Chikwe (Auxiliary Bishop Owerri), Most Rev. Solomon Amatu (Okigwe), Archbishop Anthony Obinna (Owerri), Governor Uzodinma, Most Rev. Lucius Ugorji (Umuahia and Ahiara), Most Rev. Augustine Ukwuoma (Orlu), and Most Rev. Austine Echema (Aba) after a courtesy visit to Governor Uzodinma of Imo State, at the Government House Owerri recently.

Herdsmen want to wipe out Igbos

- Archbishop raises alarm, charges Uzodinma, others to defend Igbos

Okigwe diocese thrown into mourning as Fr. Kingsley Diaku passes on

Pope Francis appoints Auxiliary Bishop for Umuahia Diocese

EDO: More mudslinging as APC chieftain blasts Oshiomhole

PPPRA backtracks, say marketers can't fix fuel price

NDDC: N'Delta agitators back NASS over N40bn probe

Vanguard

MONDAY, JUNE 8, 2020

N200

IPOB waging war against Nigeria — PRESIDENCY

• Says group using false allegations of persecution of Christians
• Adds IPOB wants to drive wedge between FG and UK, US allies

Big trouble, as more Nigerians sink deeper into poverty

• Population of poor expected to hit 89.5 million
• Poverty worsening as population growth outpaces GDP

NIGERIANS BELOW POVERTY LINE (2016-2020) IN MILLIONS

A-Ibom community deserted as cultists kill 2

Oil thieves gun down NSDC personnel in Rivers

Outrage greets Miyetti Allah's 'Nigeria belongs to Fulani' comment

Fulani herdsmen kill 32 in Kogi State attack

Senate faults court order, asks CJN to caution judicial officers

TheGuardian

Conscience, Nurtured by Truth

Herdsmen kill 50 in Benue communities

The PUNCH

86 killed as herds... attack 11 Plateau ...

Six injured, 50 hou...

Plateau places three LGA...

Vanguard

Soludo, Yakassai, Balarabe, Reps flay FG's economic policies

Again, herdsmen invade Enugu, kill seminarian

Infinix
NOTE4

NIGERIA CHRISTIANS
ARE
UNDER ATTACK:
Buhari Act NOW!

OMG

11:01 PM
PHOTO NEWS: Inside the...
www.premiumtimesng.com
SHARE
Menu
PHOTO NEWS: Inside the massive extrajudicial killings in Nigeria's South-East
Save
click here to close

NIGERIA CHRISTIANS
ARE
UNDER ATTACK:
Buhari Act NOW!

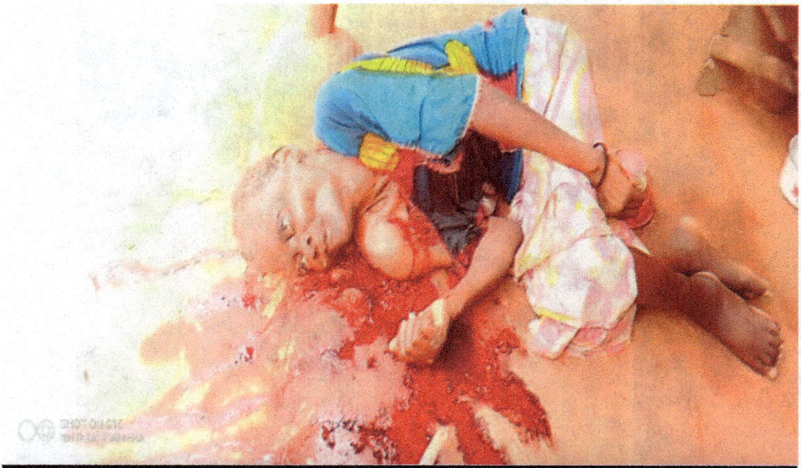

Chisom Stephen Blessing
14 Sep 2017 at 6:25 am •

A video showing soldiers of the Nigerian army torturing men believed to be members of the Indigenous People of Biafra (IPOB) has surfaced on social media.

10:36

BIAFRAN HEROS FROM SLAVERY

Olaedo Ikwuano of Usakka

Around the year 1745, in the village of Usakka Ikwuano (four kindreds) clans one early morning, precisely few moments after their parents had joined other able bodied men and women of the clan to go to the farms, slave raiders silently entered a compound and discretely caught and muzzled two pre-teen siblings. A boy and a girl.

The raiders had watched the village for two days before launching that attack. They know children were well trained to hide away once the adults leave the homestead, and can send secret calls to their parents once slave raiders were spotted. So these type of attacks were swift and desperate. The slave traffickers started by tiptoeing into one of the major compounds in the enclave almost as soon as the last adult walked around that old Ngwu tree at the eastern approach to the village. One of the men had selected the compound for a first attack by chance.

The boy was walking out with the intention of climbing his favorite *ube* to pluck ripe fruits when he came face to face with the terrible presence of a slave raider at the back exit of his grandfather's compound. He turned and ran back inside the compound intending to dash into the obi. But the slave raider was faster than him. He caught one of the boy's flailing hands yanked on it with force immediately dislocating the arm at the shoulder while dragging the boy down with him. At the same time expertly covering the boy's mouth as he was going to scream. The younger girl realizing what was happening, made it to the far end of the low walls of the fence and vaulted it without problem; but she landed just next to the waiting presence of two slave raiders. By the time she completed the first step, she found herself lifted bodily up and was put into the gaping mouth of a jute bag. The bag moved as the raiders took off dragging and half carrying the bag. She was aware when the company descended the little depression towards the last years farming fields, before she lost consciousness. They raiders ran all day without stopping. Then they halted and took out the girl from the bag. One of the men reset the boy's arm, instantly bringing him relief from the pain he had been nursing ever since that struggle in his grandfather's compound. The two children were the only kidnapped victims for that day. The party continued the escape flight after a few minutes rest. By midnight, they had not entered any village but walked carefully away from homesteads in their nefarious business pattern. They let the two children sit down as they finally stopped for a longer rest. The boy shunted closer to his sister and took her weak hands in his and both began to cry.

Olaudah (or just most probably OLAEDOH a word which means 'GOLD' in local language) was sold and resold more than six times before he found himself at the Ocean-front bound for that journey of no return. He had lost sight of his sister the very next day following their kidnapping, after she was sold, but they had been united for a day within the months before he arrived at that Ocean.

Because of his young age, all his masters kept him more as a house-pet than as a slave. They used him as companions to their own children. Finally, in London, he trained as a ship's cabin boy and a sailor. Then his master decided to send him to school. Olaedoh Ikwuano was later to earn his keep and went on to buy his freedom. He wrote many books and campaigned for abolition of slavery.

Olaedoh Ikwuano used the teachings of religion to argue for human equality. Economically, he stated that slavery was destroying African society; impoverishing the continent and destroying the society in its entirety. He used his ability to achieve financial freedom to show that Africans are capable of attaining every level of human success intellectually, morally and otherwise. He was able to turn his book into a success when the mainstream British publishing companies refused to publish for him. They sought to stop his story out of discrimination. Ikwuano in response sold his book before publication by the method of subscription to copies. He went around selling a promissory note to deliver his book after publication and through this method raised enough money needed to self-publish his book. He followed the promise through and was a tremendous financial success with his book much to the dismay of publishing houses of the day.

I heard the story of Olaedoh from a University professor who in the early 1990's was using his works to trace the natural origins of Olaedoh as being present day Ussaka in Ikwuano in Biafra land. Olaudah among other abolitionists of his age was credited with jinggering the eventual law that abolished slavery in the world however, he died on March 31, 1797, ten years before slavery was abolished in the UK by King George the III in 1807.

Sarah Forbes

A baby girl was born to the king of Oke-Odan in 1843, there was much rejoicing in the kingdom, for the birth of a child is always seen as a blessing from the God of the earth to her parents and the community. In this instance this baby was a special blessing to one of the youngest wives of the King following a treaty with a neighboring kingdom. The marriage was necessitated by the need to form an alliance and strengthen both kingdoms because they thought that Dahomey was tittering on the brink of collapse in power and influence. Barely 5 years later, Dahomey rallied, invaded and destroyed Oke-Odan. In the war, the royal family of Oke -Odan was wiped out, the little girl was taken with all other citizens of Oke-Odan as spoils of war. Many of the inhabitants of Oke-Odan were sold into slavery; King Ghezo kept the girl. During a meeting with the British envoy to his kingdom, Ghezo presented the little girl as a gift to the envoy Captain Frederick E. Forbes.

It was recorded, Captain Forbes accepted the gift because he believed the girl would meet worse fate at the hands of her captors who were then not convinced to end slavery as an economic venture. The captain renamed Aina Omoba as Sarah Forbes Bonetta and received her on behalf of the British monarch of the time: Queen Victoria. The queen later sent Sarah aged eight years, to be educated at a school in Sierra leone, west Africa, The queen believed that the British climate was the cause of a very bad cough Sarah had developed. Sarah returned to England in 1855 when she was 12 years old, and became a companion to the queen who had developed a fondness for her. She appeared regularly with the queen in public not as a slave but as a companion. She was later permitted to marry a wealthy Yoruba businessman Captain James Pinson Labulo Davies in 1862 at the age of 19. Sarah Forbes Bonetta died at the young age of 37 in 1880.

King Jaja of Opobo

He was born at Umuduruoha Amaigbo and named Mbanaso Okwaraozurumba. He was the third son of his parents. Igbo ancestral villages survived by maintaining good alliances with their neighbors and by the ability to withstand foreign invasion from enemies. Igbo communities easily go to war against each other over cases like murder, rape, assault committed against a member of a village by a member of another village. Therefore, manpower is jealously guarded. Children are a big resource to the family, even the practice of polygamy was primarily to raise a large family and ensure survival of all, by the efforts of many hands. Therefore, history that Mbanaso, a third son of the family was sold by his family is false. It makes more sense that he was caught and sold into slavery by his father's enemy when he was twelve years of age.

He served his masters very well and grew in wisdom and intelligence. He was later sold to Chief Alali, the head of Opubo Annie Pepple Royal house. What worked for "Jaja" was not only his wisdom, his intelligence or his entrepreneurial skills. It was his ability to take risks. He was very brave and determined when he had decided on what to do. Above all, Jaja was immensely compassionate and has a human touch to go with his business sense.

At the death of his master Alali, the position of the head of the Anna Pepple royal house became vacant, every eligible chief of the house did not want to assume authority because of debts owed by the former head. Jaja knew that if the house was broken up, there would be hardship for all its members. Control of businesses and day to day running would become unpredictable, loss of livelihood and probably a descent to lawlessness may result. So he took up the challenge to be the head of Anna Pepple. However, few years later when Jaja had paid out the debts and raised the house through successful business activity, other chiefs rose up against him. Finally he left Anna Pepple house and moved away to nearby Opobo town to establish his own 'House'. Jaja organized Opobo into a kingdom and a trading community. Opobo crowned him king. For many years, he withstood European forces trying to take complete control of trading activities in the delta. He was a fair judge, a good king, and was immensely loved by his people. With growth in economic activities, the kingdom grew tremendously, but the British tricked him onto a war ship with the promise of negotiation. Jaja was immediately arrested and deported to West indies. After a few years of imprisonment, they poisoned him on a fake voyage to bring him home to Opobo.

King Jaja saw the evils of Christianity as a means of manipulation and so rejected it. But he not only accepted western education, he built schools and caused his people to be educated. King Jaja was killed because he possessed a rare wisdom and intelligence and because he would not allow Britain to indoctrinate and colonize his people.

We face great decisions of our lives, which will definitely affect our individual and collective destinies down the generations. It is pertinent that in this age and time we live in troubled times, we should be courageous, determined and brave to stand up to the times, to fight for our right to existence. It is true we must fight for ourselves, no one would fight our battles for us. Yes, many may be kind, offer us assistance or in the event that those who are charged by the world bodies feel morally or legally justified, they would give us justice. Nevertheless, in the world we live in, through centuries of history we know if we do not fight for our right to live free, we would be annihilated and consigned to the pages of history if ever.

News from Biafra

The United Kingdom High Commissioner to Nigeria quits Twitter.

Catriona Liang the United Kingdom High Commissioner to Nigeria have reportedly taken a leave from twitter. In a post she made 6 days ago, Catriona tweeted: I am on leave and taking a break from Twitter. See you on my return. Best wishes Catriona. Catriona had in recent weeks and months being the subject of angst by Nigerians over her activities in Nigeria, which had come across as completely disrespectful and totally unwelcome to Nigerians. She had embarked on tours to security establishments, been seen meeting with governors and military chiefs who would launch unnecessary crackdowns against Nigerians from the Lekki SARS protests shootings, the Obigbo massacres in Portharcourt and along Northeastern Nigeria where terrorists are on the rampage. She had also been seen bringing British forces into Nigeria, but all these instances would lead to further killings by security forces against indigenous people. Therefore, all her postings on twitter had been met with criticisms, ridicule and curses against her and against United Kingdom.

Biafran Memorial Day 31st May 2021

Tensions were high on Sunday, 31st of May, 2021 in southern Nigeria as Biafrans remembered estimated more than 3 million people who died in the Biafra war of 1966-1970.

They activated the new normal "sit at home" for Biafra memorial day have become a standard for Eastern Nigeria every 29th to 31st of May since 2014. The Indigenous People of Biafra (IPOB), and the Movement for the Actualization of the Sovereign State of Biafra (MASSOB), which are the leading separatist groups, remembered war victims over two days. The event started with a candlelight march on Sunday evening, followed by a strict order for people to remain indoors on Monday for their own safety.

"Every person in Biafraland was advised to observe a sit-at-home order on Monday," IPOB spokesman Emma Powerful said in a statement, noting that markets and shops must be closed for those days.

"We strongly advise our people against flouting this order as anyone found outside one's house that day may be the target of our enemies," he said, alluding to federal security forces.

The streets of Owerri, the capital of Imo state, were deserted on Sunday. "

That same Sunday, the police alleged that six gunmen shot dead an influential politician, Ahmed Gulak, in Owerri, Imo state. Gulak, an advisor to former Nigerian president Goodluck Jonathan, had been on his way to the airport when he was killed. The Indeginous people had vehemently condemned the killing of Ahmed Gulak, calling it a calculated attempt at demonizing Biafrans. It must be noted that Gulak has in recent days totally supported Biafra, by openly making videos sent online which condemned 'shoot at sight' stance of the IGP and the recklessness of the Buhari government in not negotiating with Nigerian youths and Biafran agitators. IPOB leader, Mazi Nnamdi Kanu, also condemned the killing calling it a witch-hunt.

In relation to the memorial day, many pictures and videos shared online in all social media platforms showed deserted roads, streets and markets, calling it a 'complete lockdown'. Neighboring states of Abia, Akwa-ibom, Delta, Cross-river, Ebonyi, Anambra and Bayelsa states were also on edge, with witnesses reporting that main thoroughfares, streets and roads were deserted. All establishments; banks, hospitals, schools and businesses were closed, only Nigerian military vehicles could be seen patrolling a few hotspots in Owerri.

In 1967, following a bloody coup d'etat, ethnic Hausa and Fulani and other Northern ethnic groups blamed ethnic Igbos for the death of heads of governments and so launched a sustained bloody pogroms that led to the killings of more than 30,000 Igbos resident in Northern Nigeria by the police, army and the other ethnic groups in Northern Nigeria. Remaining ethnic Igbos who were able to run, left Northern Nigeria for their eastern homeland. The Failure of then Nigerian leader Gowon to implement an agreed peace accord led to the declaration of independence for the "Republic of Biafra," sparking a bloody civil which killed over 3 million Igbos in three years mostly due to economic blockade enforced by Nigeria and Cameroun against Biafra.

Sustained attacks and extra-judicial killings by the combined police, civil defense, army teams and by armed killer-Fulani-herdsmen across eastern states of Nigeria.

On Sunday the 31st of May 2021, while Biafrans were in somber mood remembering the genocide of 1966-1970 and the ongoing military killings sanctioned by Muhamadu Buhari, killer-Fulani herdsmen attacked more than 4 communities of Tologa, Odoken, Ndiobasi, and Obakotara in Ebonyi State killing over 30 people, women and children included. There were another 12 people in the neighboring state reportedly massacred at Ado Local Government Area of Benue state by the same killer-Fulani herdsmen.

Both Ado in Benue state and the communities attacked in Ebonyi are ethnic Igbos separated by state boundaries alone. Uchenna Okpokwu, a resident of the area said the invaders came with guns and matchets. There were graphic videos of bodies cut in pieces and several survivors with matchet wounds being stitched up in a hospital. Confirming the attacks, house of representative member, representing the affected districts, complained about the latent inability of the security forces in halting incessant attacks against indigenous people by invading killer-Fulani herdsmen.

In Nwori community of Ebonyi state, pictures showed injured women and children lying helpless in a health clinic; they had matchet cuts to the head and all over their bodies and legs. An accompanying video related that several young babies were raped in front of their wounded mothers after their fathers had been killed. An injured mother showed a terrible anal injury in her one year-old child.

Similarly, suspected killer-Fulani herdsmen attacked Ekpoffo in Eha-Amufu community in Isi-Uzo Local government area of Ebonyi state and slaughtered four persons leaving another seven with serious injuries.

At Afor-Enyiogugu Mbaise five people were shot and killed by the police and army joint team. This news was obtained from graphic video circulated online showing two bodies being hurriedly taken in two different motorcycles for evacuation to a nearby hospital, another showed two victims with broken legs. Yet another video showed a victim with gunshots to his stomach being led away for possible treatment, they were looking for means of transport to the hospital.

On Saturday 30th of May 2021, the Nigerian military responding to the order of the IGP went to Owerri hostel of the Imo state university and opened fire, killing about 15 students and abducting many more. On the same day 30th May, a video showed travelers fleeing bandit attack along Tegina-Zugero highway in Niger state

News about Nigeria

Gunmen seized at least 136 students from an Islamic school in Tegina town in Niger state. According to the owner of an Islamic school, no fewer than 136 students had been abducted from Tegina's Salihu Tanko Islamic School, Tegina town, Niger State Nigeria, on Sunday 30th May 2021. Grieving parents are currently pleading with Nigerian authorities to step up efforts to save the students kidnapped by the gunmen. Meanwhile, a Niger state police spokesperson said the latest kidnapping was carried out by "armed bandits on board motorcycles in their numbers". The gunmen fired "indiscriminately and abducted a yet to be ascertained number of children", he said, adding that the gunmen shot one person dead in the process. Authorities said "tactical teams" have been mobilized to rescue the students, while a fighter jet was sent to fly over the area to try to spot the kidnappers and the abductees.

Mohammed Garba, the father of an abducted student while waiting for news about his child outside the school, said: "We want the authorities to do more,"

Meanwhile, Niger state's Deputy Governor Ahmed Mohammed Ketso ruled out any payment to the kidnappers.

Since December 2020, gangs of so-called bandits seeking lucrative ransom have kidnapped more than 700 students during raids on boarding schools and other educational facilities across northern Nigeria in several incidents.

Sheik Gumi an Islamic teacher have been involved in negotiations and payment of ransom to these criminal gangs. He had gone so far as to say that the ransom payments were merited by the bandits since they live in the bushes.

On Saturday, 14 students from a university in northwestern Nigeria were freed, after having spent 40 days in captivity.

In another related incident, kidnappers had freed 29 students abducted in Nigeria's Kaduna state after the parents of the students sold properties to raise up to 180 million naira in ransom money. This they paid to the bandits, there are reports, some of the demands of the kidnappers included purchases of dozens of motorcycles for them. The readiness of the Nigerian security to curtail incidents of kidnapping and banditry comes into question; seeing that motorcycles are the bandits' preferred mode of transportation.

There is no security across the nation, so attackers have ample opportunities to seize a lot people. The bandits know negotiating with the government will result in either amnesty or ransom being paid. Meanwhile Nigerian security forces are deployed to eastern Nigeria to kill and terrorize indigenous people who refused to hand over their lands to bandits.

At least $18.34m have been paid to kidnappers as ransom – mostly by families and the government – between June 2011 and March 2020, according to a report by SB Morgen (SBM) Intelligence, a Lagos-based political risk analysis firm.

Sowore shot and wounded

Nigerian police dispersing a crowd of protesters on Monday in the capital Abuja, have shot and injured Sowore; the protest which was called against the IGP's order to the Military to shoot and kill Igbos was under way with many people present, when activist Omoyele Sowore, a well-known opposition figure who has organized previous protests against bad governance said he was wounded by a police officer.

Sowore posted a picture of a wound on Twitter but Nigerian police have denied the reports that he was shot, saying there was "no record of such incident" at this time, police spokeswoman Mariam Yusuf said.

Another activist said he saw Sowore being shot with a teargas canister live on Facebook. In a face book post we could hear the words of activist Inibehe Effiong on the video posted on Twitter. "Sowore has just been shot by a female police officer... She fired a teargas cannister directly at Sowore,"

One of his lawyers Marshall Abubakar told AFP he had been rushed to hospital. "I am with him at the (hospital) theatre now trying to ascertain, but it is a serious injury, a serious wound, a serious penetration," said Abubakar.

Amnesty International Nigeria said it had received a "disturbing report that activist Omoyele Sowore was shot by the police, protesters deserved to be listened to, not shot at. We call on Nigerian authorities to investigate the incident and bring perpetrators to justice," the rights groups wrote on Twitter.

Nigerian authorities arrested Sowore on December 31, severely beating him according to another of his lawyers, Femi Falana. The police officers who arrested Sowore "subjected him to severe beating and left him with bruises all over his body," Falana told AFP.

Insecurity in Plateau state and genocide of the Irigwe nation

A total of 40 persons of Irigwe ethnic nationality in Plateau State have been reportedly killed in attacks by killer-Fulani herdsmen in the Bassa and Jos North local government areas of the state in the past four months. The National President of Irigwe Development Association, Robert Dodo, disclosed this at a press conference in Jos on Tuesday. Dodo also said 20 houses belonging to the natives and over 500 cultivated farmlands worth over N1bn were destroyed during the period under review.

Giving a breakdown of the attacks and the names of victims, the National President noted that the killings started at Dudun Maiyanga village with the murder of two people on February 2, 2021. The herdsmen, escalated the attacks to 15 other villages, including Zirshe, Kishosho, Rikwe-Chongo, Ntireku, Nchenyu, Kamaru, Ribakwa, Dong, Rafiki, Nkienhie, Kpachudu, as well as Ncha.

According to Dodo, in spite of the series of unabated attacks in Irigwe land, they had received no serious attention from those whose primary responsibility was to secure the lives and property of the people.

"We are pained and have been allowed to mourn and grieve on our own as if we don't have a government. "What is happening in Irigwe land is nothing short of genocide and ethnic cleansing orchestrated by the Fulani to wipe away the entire Irigwe tribe or if this seems unachievable, to depopulate their number with the aim of taking over their ancestral land.

We are concerned because our people have been confined to internally displaced camps (IDP's) in a continuous brutal show of force by the Fulani militia against the Irigwe people and nobody has been arrested, investigated or prosecuted according to the law of the nation. We are worried because without enforcing security measures government is encouraging criminality," the National President lamented. As a way of stopping further attacks on the people, Dodo called on the government to prevail on the Fulani herdsmen to suspend open grazing in their domain.

A 30-year-old woman has been allegedly raped, while searching for a shop to rent in Ogun State. The victim was reportedly raped by a 42-year-old man, John Daniel, who had offered to help her get a large metal container to use as a shop. The Police Public Relations Officer in the state, DSP Abimbola Oyeyemi, disclosed this in a statement on Monday. Oyeyemi said the suspect was arrested on Sunday by men of the command for forcefully having carnal knowledge of the woman. He said the suspect was arrested following a complaint lodged at the Sango-Ota Divisional Headquarters by the victim.

Oyeyemi stated, "It was reported that she (victim) went in search of a shop to rent for her business. Around 6 pm when she met the suspect, who told her that there was a container kept in his care by someone, which she could rent or purchase and use as a shop. The suspect took the lady to his house and asked the victim to sit down in his living room for him to call the owner of the said container. He however, locked the door and brought out a screw-driver and a bottle with which he threatened her. She was raped after being beaten mercilessly.

The desperate lack of jobs and opportunities in Nigeria have been described as a situation, which had repeatedly led to increase in crime especially against women. It is also the cause of violent crimes among youth who have been rendered hopeless by ineffective government policies. Just like in the case above, we remember the tragic murder of Iniobiong Umoren, who was out looking for a job in Uyo. The job seeker was raped, killed and buried in a shallow grave by the man who invited her for a job interview three weeks ago. The story was that Umoren, a graduate of the

University of Uyo, Akwa Ibom, had last month indicated that she was looking for a job on Twitter. She was invited for a job interview by a man who contacted her on Twitter to an undisclosed location along airport road in Uyo. She was allegedly raped and murdered by her abductor, Uduak Frank Akpan, who later buried her in a shallow grave.

Gunmen Kills Kogi State Commissioner, Kidnap LG Chairman.
Further evidence of the rising insecurity in the country is an attack by yet to be identified bandits who killed a Kogi state Commissioner on Tuesday. The armed gunmen killed a Commissioner in the Kogi State Pension Board, Mr Solomon Akeweje, and abducted the Chairman of Yagba West Local Government, Mr Pius Kolawole. Spokesman of the state police command, DSP William Aya, who confirmed the incident told the News Agency of Nigeria (NAN) that the Commissioner and Kolawole were travelling in the same vehicle when they were attacked at about 4:30 pm of Saturday, May 1. The police spokesman said that the victims were attacked at Eruku, a border community between Kwara and Kogi States. According to Aya, both Akeweje and Kolawole were travelling back to Egbe from Kwara State when they were attacked by yet-to-be-identified gunmen. The whereabouts of the abducted Kolawole is unknown as at the time of this report while his abductors are yet to call. The driver of the vehicle survived the attack while the corpse of Akeweje was deposited at the morgue of ECWA Hospital, Egbe.

Criminality increases when there is presumed lack of accountability by the people who wield power in a failing state.
On Sunday May 25th 2021, a Nigerian soldier was arrested by the police after he allegedly murdered a businessman who gave him lift and then stole his car. The soldier was arrested by the Akwa Ibom State Police command in Ikot Abasi Local government area of the state.

It was gathered that the army officer allegedly killed the businessman then dispossessed him of his vehicle after receiving him a ride on Sunday, May 23. A source from Ikot Abasi LGA told 'The Nation Newspaper' that the suspected officer was tracked and arrested at Ukanafun LGA on Tuesday, May 25, the vehicle, including a rifle were recovered from him.

"The incident happened on Sunday; a motorist offered a serving army officer a ride in his vehicle, not knowing that he was going to kill him. When they got to a lonely stretch of road, the army officer attacked and killed the business man and dumped his corpse by the way side," the source said.

On Monday, the deceased relatives came to the police in Ikot Abasi for assistance. The vehicle had a tracking device, so the police assisted them in tracking the vehicle. They tracked the car to Ukanafun LGA, where they surrounded a hotel and arrested the army officer, they then recovered the vehicle, and an AK-47 rifle from him. Spokesperson of the command, Odiko Macdon, confirmed the incident, adding that the matter is still under investigation, "we are trying to get conclusive reports and determine the identity of the persons involved," he added.

Exclusive interview of Mazi Nnamdi Kalu by David Nyekorah Matsunga of the Punchline Africa TV.

The interview which took place today the 21st of May 2021, was relayed across every internet platform, and beamed live in East Africa and many other nations, Mazi Nnamdi Kalu went into details to state the case for Biafra. Mazi Nnamdi Kalu gave a detailed lesson to the world on why the Indigenous people of Nigeria are agitating for self-determination: bad governance, which stems from ethnic chauvinism, corruption, religious intolerance and blatant disregard to the rule of Law that have been going on in Nigeria for as long as Nigeria was constituted.

He emphasized therefore that the present structure of Nigeria is untenable and this was giving lee way for proliferation of terrorism, like Boko Haram, Islamic State of West Africa Province (ISWAP), Fulani herdsmen, Bandits and Mitatti Allah groups.

David Matsunga asked the leader of IPOB to address African union directly by sending a message to Kenyan president, Uhuru Kenyata, who is the present head of the peace and security in African Union, a member of United Nations Security council representing sub-saharan Africa and with the knowledge of the hundreds of indigenous peoples seeking asylum in eastern Africa. Mazi Nnamdi Kalu has this to say: "I want to let the African Union, the world and everyone listening to know that contrary to the lies and misinformation from Nigeria, Biafra is not against prosperity in Africa, but our agitation is an indication of the decay in Nigeria." He went on to inform the world that the disintegration of Nigeria will however strengthen African Union's worth, power, relevance and value before the comity of nations. He insisted that Nigeria have suppressed thoughts, wisdom and development of human resources especially in Biafraland, as an example he pointed out that the attorney general of the federation in a secular nation is a Sharia judge who have no knowledge of legal principles. The interviewer remembered that the said attorney general was the one who gave a reason to court that termites ate his legal notes.

Mazi Nnamdi kanu likened Nigeria to a 'cancer' eating away at the African body and preventing progress, growth and development into the future for the peoples and the nations of Africa. That Nigeria by running on nepotism, lies and corruption ends up corrupting everyone. At this stage he gave example that private oil companies doing business in Nigeria end up being corrupted and drawn into a vicious circle of corruption and irresponsible business strategies to the detriment of the nation. This has also affected diplomatic corps becoming corrupt and making no objective reports to their own countries about the true state of affairs in Nigeria.

Mazi Nnamdi Kalu reminded the world that in other to maintain its oppression of indigenous people the Inspector General of Police have relocated his forces to Biafra and gave a direct order to the military to kill all Biafrans, with the supposed support of the United kingdom Ambassador Cariona Liang.

Mazi Nnamdi Kalu gave his dream of what Biafra would be as a home for every Biafran regardless of their different national differences. A nation where everyone would be a free citizen with equal rights with every other Biafran. A home that encourages innovation, growth, ideas, talent and skill development in all fields of human endeavor. A nation where police would not bear arms, a republican nation that would attract inward investment, no rancor, where every black man would be an honorary citizen and then Europe would realize that Africa can achieve greatness with its own efforts.

The interview extended to very difficult topics and compared the lives of both the interviewer and the IPOB leader during years in exile and loss of family members. There was also a latent undertone throughout the interview that Africa need the freedom of its peoples from oppressive policies and destructive ethnic ideologies, from age old divide and rule tactics that is further impoverishing Africa to the delight and profit of Europe and other continents.

Online commentators had great praise for the professionalism of the Punchline Africa Tv, through the vibrant interviewer. They expressed delight that this interview brings to light the true position of indigenous peoples in Nigeria. All Biafrans who commented praised the resolve of the IPOB leader and all of them expressed complete support to the aspiration for an independent Biafran Nation.

Anti-open grazing resolution by 17 southern Governors.

About eight states of southern Nigeria have set in motion steps to give legal backing to a complete ban on open grazing in the region. This comes after the recent meeting of the state governors under the umbrella of the southern Governors Forum held at Asaba the capital of Delta state last week. The states include Akwa Ibom, Ondo, Enugu, Edo, Imo, Ogun, Delta and Anambra. In the communique released after the said meeting, the governors strongly called for a total ban of open grazing in their territories. Their resolution have received wide endorsement from the people of the affected states.

The Igbo sociopolitical organization Ohanaeze Ndigbo have declared full support for the governors resolution. Mr. Alex Ogbonna, National publicity secretary of Ohanaeze told reporters that the resolution of the governors would go a long way in dealing with prolonged cases of destruction of farmlands by cattle and livestock herders. He also pointed that herders have been allowed to carry guns over the years, which gives them courage to attack villages with impunity. It must be noted that many of these states already have anti-open grazing laws but these laws were ineffective because of lack of commitment on the part of the police enforcement.

The speaker Ekiti state house of assembly, said that with the federal government's recalcitrant posture on state police creation, the enforcement of the Ekiti states' 'Prohibition of cattle and other ruminants grazing law 2016' was impossible.

In Abia state, the Control of Normadic cattle rearing and prohibition of grazing routes/reserves law 2018; restricts transportation of livestock to rail or road haulage but this have been largely ignored by police and other federal security agencies.

The federal government's refusal to enforce these laws have led to the accusation that Fulani herdsmen who carry heavy assault weapons, assault and sometimes kill farmers if they complain about destruction of their farms by the herders' animals are protected and maybe out rightly encouraged to sack indigenous villages in Nigeria.

Despite this, the eight states and others are now set to enact anti-open grazing laws following the pronouncement of the 17 governors.

Mass migration of Northern youths to Eastern states of Nigeria have continued unabated.

The police and the civil defense force have again intercepted a Dangote Trailer transporting hundreds of Fulani youths to eastern Nigeria. This has continued to cause alarm and fear in the Biafran homelands. In a video that had gone viral, a Dangote trailer which was missing its plate number, was stopped by police for routine check. The driver informed the police that he was carrying bags of salt however, on inspection of the trailer, policemen were shocked to see hundreds of Fulani men. The driver was eventually ordered to drive back to wherever they were coming from.

Mass migrations of this kind are unprecedented in Nigeria especially as the Fulani youths all have no single item of luggage or money for their upkeep with them, nor can they state why they are going to the east, where they intend to go and how they will fend for themselves.

News from Nigeria

The Military knows where the bandits' base are.

Alhaji Lai Mohammed, the minister of Information has revealed that the Nigerian military knows where the bandits' bases are. He said that the insinuation that Nigerian government was clueless was unfounded but that the federal government is only being careful. In an assurance to the media, Lai Mohammed said that though the government is facing challenges, it is not overwhelmed, only trying to be careful to avoid civilian casualties. He assured all Nigerians that the government acknowledges the security challenges it faces at this time, from terrorism to kidnapping, banditry and farmer herder conflicts but that they would confront these challenges in the days ahead.

It is noteworthy that the government of President Muhamadu Buhari has failed in all aspects of nation building with the exception of empty promises. These statements of Lai Mohamed are seen by media commentators as one of the many lies peddled by the Information minister once he stands before the media. Lai Mohammed had assured Nigerians that Boko Haram had been defeated so many times before, until he coined the word constructively defeated. Lai Mohammed had assured Nigeria most recently that there would be no fuel-pump price increase only for the price to be doubled a few days later. Lai Mohammed had assured Nigerians of economic stability and political stability and they are waiting for it many years later.

Ibori loot returned to Nigeria

5.8 million Dollars recovered by United Kingdom agencies that was stolen by a former Nigerian state governor and laundered in Britain have now been returned to Nigeria, the Nigerian authorities say. Former Delta state Governor James Ibori was convicted of money laundering in the UK in 2012. Prosecutors say he stole an estimated 165 million dollars from the coffers of Delta state. A Bombadier Challenger jet, is among the items listed in court documents for a confiscation order against Ibori. 4.2 million pounds were recovered from Ibori's wife, sister and fiduciary agent who were also convicted of money laundering. Mr. David Ugolor, the director,

African Network on environmental and economic justice regretted that the money had not been returned to the state from where it was stolen but to the country.

Impeachment Proceedings dispute at the Nigerian senate

Senators elected on the platform of the People's Democratic Party (PDP) and the All Progressive Congress (APC) on Wednesday last faced off over moves to begin impeachment proceedings against president Muhammadu Buhari. Senator Enyinnaya Abaribe, the senates' minority leader had listed various constitutional breaches on which basis, the minority caucus of the National assembly was ready to impeach the President. According to him these breaches includes: failure to guarantee security and welfare of the nation as being the primary purpose of government. In support during plenary session, Senator Biodun Olujimi, urged her colleagues not to hesitate in instituting impeachment proceedings. However, Yususf Yusuf APC senator from Taraba Central rejected Olujimi's call stating that impeachment of the President would leave the Vice president in power or if further argued would devolve power to the senate president. He argued, that this still keeps power in the same political party being accused of cluelessness. The matter could not generate enough support as the two political party representatives supported their sides, however Olujimi stated that when the matter is placed squarely on the table, the Senators would think seriously about it.

African Finance Summit in France

President Muhammadu Buhari on Sunday 16th May 2021, departed Abuja en-route Paris, France for a four day official visit to France. While there, he attended the African Finance Summit which focussed on reviewing African economy impacted by the Coronavirus pandemic. The summit on Tuesday 18th May 2021, had agreed to work towards persuading richer nations to reallocate about 100 billion dollars in IMF special drawing rights monetary reserves to African states. This, it is expected aims at improving Covid 19 vaccine rollout. Even though the communique addressed financing needs in support of sustainable green recovery and enhanced private sector driven growth, but it sets out no policy routes to achieving such goals. The Senegalese President has called the agreement reached, a new start, a new deal. However, the fact remains that most of the attending leaders of Africa are dictators, shielded from the reality of their nation's economy either by design or choice, and the latent lack of political will to better the lot of their nations.

Muhamadu Buhari took over a Nigerian economy that had risen to the best in African under Goodluck Ebele Jonathan and Ngozi Okonjo Iweala as finance minister in 2015. Today he has rubbished it to become the poverty capital of the world. He has refused to tackle insecurity, refused to listen to dissenting views, divided the nation along ethnic and religious lines and has no clue as to what is a president's function. Therefore his participation in France Summit does not give Nigerians any iota of assurance or hope at all.

Bandits kidnap foreigner in Niger state.

Bandits have killed two soldiers and abducted a foreigner in the Magama Local Government Area of Niger state Nigeria. It was gathered that this happened on Monday the 17th of May 2021. The Fulani criminals attacked the Libale community in Nasko and were repulsed. Two soldiers were killed in the shootout, but they also caught the Chinese national and took him with them. Security agents are presently combing the mountain area and forests hoping to apprehend the bandits. The Chinese man was said to be a staff of a construction firm involved in road development in the area.

In a related development, Gunmen have invaded a sharia court in Bauren Zakat village in Safana Local Government Area of Katsina state and Kidnapped a Judge Identified as Alhaji Husaini Sama'ila. This happened on Tuesday 18th May 2021 at about 3pm. In confirming the incident, The Katsina Police Public relations office SP, Gambo Isah expressed shock as to which assignment could have taken the judge to work on that day. It can be recalled that the Juniour staff union (JUSUN) Katsina state was in an industrial action against the state presently. Again Gambo said that the court was relocated from the area to Safana due to security issues, therefore the Judge must really have a personal issue to be there when the bandits attacked.

Updated News items as compiled today 19th April 2021

News from Biafra

Prison Break in Owerri the Imo state Capital

Nigeria (Reuters) - More than 1,800 prisoners are on the run in southeast Nigeria after escaping their prison cells when heavily armed gunmen attacked their prison using explosives and rocket-propelled grenades, the authorities said.

Nigerian police said it believed a banned separatist group, the Indigenous People of Biafra (IPOB), was behind the attack in the city of Owerri, but a spokesman for the group denied involvement. The secessionist movement in the southeast is one of several serious security challenges facing President Muhammadu Buhari, including a decade-long Islamist insurgency in the northeast, a spate of school kidnappings in the northwest and piracy in the Gulf of Guinea.

Buhari said the attack, in a city near the oil-rich Niger Delta region that is the mainstay of Africa's top crude exporter and biggest economy, was an "act of terrorism". He ordered security forces to apprehend the fleeing prisoners.

The attackers stormed the facility at around 2:15 a.m. (0115 GMT) on Monday, according to the Nigerian Correctional Service said. "The Owerri Custodial Centre in Imo state has been attacked by unknown gunmen and forcefully released a total of 1,844 inmates in custody," its spokesman said in a statement late on Monday.

The police said attackers used explosives to blast the administrative block of the prison and entered the prison yard. IPOB wants independence for a region in southeast: Biafra. More than three million people died in a 1967-70 civil war between the Nigerian government and secessionists there. In recent months security in the region has deteriorated. Several police stations have been attacked since January, with large amounts of ammunition stolen. There are reports of the IPOB's paramilitary wing, the Eastern Security Network (ESN), clashing with the military. But an IPOB spokesman told Reuters the group did not carry out the prison raid.

"IPOB and ESN were not involved in the attack in Owerri, Imo state. It is not our mandate to attack security personnel or prison facilities," the IPOB spokesman said in a phone call. The state governor later absolved the IPOB and its security outfit the Eastern Security network of responsibility when after a few days following the attack the governor alleged that the culprits may have been sponsored by political enemies as vendetta to make the state ungovernable.

Dead bodies found dumped in Calabar

The Nigerian Police have cordoned off the valley where fifteen decapitated and decomposed bodies were discovered on Tuesday 13th April 2021, in the outskirts of Calabar, the Cross River State capital. The Police Commissioner Sikiru Akande has kept mum over the incident. He feigned ignorance of the incident when told that some policemen in camouflage have cordoned off the place, retorting that "policemen do not wear camouflage on Tuesdays".

He later visited the scene of the incident but has not divulged any information on who may be behind the killings, or who dumped the bodies in the valley, or even who the victims might be.

The Nigeria Security and Civil Defence Corps (NSCDC) confirmed that a total of fifteen bodies comprising both males and females were discovered at the said location, Alfred Mboto, Permanent Secretary, Office of State Security Adviser to the Governor denied claims of extrajudicial killing, saying the bodies may be those of cult clash victims. Some commercial motorcyclist seen at the scene claimed that this would be the second time in two months bodies were found in the same area, alleging that those behind the weird action may be known to the government.

Fulani attacks Ebonyi the second time in two weeks

Fulani herdsmen in the early hours on Monday attacked a village in Ngbo community of Ohaukwu Local Government Area of Ebonyi State. It was gathered that many have allegedly lost their lives following the deadly attack. Houses of innocent indigenes of the area were burnt down by the rampaging herdsmen in the area. Ebonyi State Government on Wednesday, last week, stated that it had put modalities in place for the setting up of 1,000 vigilante groups across the state. The attack affected Ebele village in Umuogodoakpa Community, some victims of the incident are presently taking shelter in the homes of their relatives in other villages. A week prior to this present attack, herdsmen had attacked four communities in Ishielu Local Government Area where over 25 innocent rural dwellers, were massacred in cold blood. As at the time of filling this report, no suspect has been arrested by the Ebonyi State Police Command in connection with the killing.

News from Nigeria

Agitation for a Yoruba Nation

The Aare Ona Kakanfo of Yorubaland, Aare Gani Adams, has said that majority of Yoruba people are ready for self-determination. Speaking in Ikeja, Lagos, on Wednesday at the public presentation of a book, 'Roundtable Discussion on Economy and Restructuring in Nigeria,' by the National Pilot Book, Adams noted that a "power bloc" was not ready for restructuring." The book was edited by Prof. Hassan Saliu and Mr Billy Adedamola. Adams said, "I support the popular view that we have graduated from restructuring to self-determination but the main powerful bloc is not ready. This is what Yoruba leaders are clamoring for. If Nigeria is not restructured in the next three years, the future is bleak. We have different types of restructuring; so they should know the kind of restructuring that they want. If Nigeria will be restructured, we have to borrow points from 1960 and 1963, which give room for regionalism. It also allowed the six zones to develop at their own paces. My own is self-determination, you prepare for negotiation."

The Ooni of Ife, Oba Adeyeye Ogunwusi, represented by the Alara Oodaye of Ife, Oba Segun Layade, said most of the resources in the south were being enjoyed mostly in the north. He also called for the re-introduction of history in the school curriculum. In the same vein, a Peoples Democratic Party chieftain, Chief Bode George, who was represented by Dr. Charles Akitoye said Nigeria's structure was defective, adding that the country's economy was tribalistic and north-centred.

Allegation that Nigeria printed money for allocation to states.

Edo Governor Godwin Obaseki has said he won't join issues with the Federal Government over his claim that N60 billion was printed in March to support allocation to states. Obaseki had lamented the fiscal state of the nation, stating Nigeria is in financial trouble.

While speaking at the Edo state transition committee stakeholders engagement over the weekend, he claimed the Federal Government printed money to bridge FAAC allocation. "When we got FAAC for March, the federal government printed additional N50-N60 billion to top-up for us to share," he had said. But The Nation reported on Wednesday the Federal Government faulted his claim, dismissing it as untrue. The Minister of Finance, Budget and National Planning, Zainab Ahmed, said Obaseki's claim was very sad because it was "untrue".

Reacting to the Zainab Ahmed, on Thursday, Obaseki, through his official twitter handle, said: "We believe it is our duty to offer useful advice for the benefit of our country "The Minister of Finance, Budget and National Planning, @ZShamsuna should rally Nigerians to stem the obvious fiscal slide facing our country. "Rather than play the Ostrich, we urge the government to take urgent steps to end the current monetary rascality so as to prevent the prevailing economic challenge from degenerating further.

"We believe it is imperative to approach the Nigerian project with all sense of responsibility and commitment and not play to the gallery because ultimately time shall be the judge of us all."

In a turn of events, just yesterday, Godwin Emefiele, the governor of Central Bank of Nigeria (CBN) has confirmed that the Federal Government printed money to augment March 2021 allocation to states. He argued, just as he did in January when Fitch made the same accusation, that printing money to support states is not new and that 'people should stop adding coloration to it'. As if telling the states that they asked for the difficult route, Emefiele said they must be ready to pay back the loans. Emefiele explained in a video and report by TNG, that the bank's interventions are meant to address the grim economic outlook because "Nigeria is unfortunately in a very bad situation,"

The anniversary of Chibok Kidnapping

Wednesday 14th of April, 2021 made it exactly seven years since the abduction of the 276 students from the Government Girls' Secondary School, Chibok, Borno State in North-East Nigeria. But today there are 112 of the girls still in the captivity at the hands of Boko Haram terrorists.

On that night of April 14, 2014, terrorists invaded the Government Girls Secondary School, Chibok, and by day break a total of 276 students were found to had been taken away. Many people in Nigeria and around the world thought the news was fake and an impossible feat until the terrorists released a chilling video showing majority of the girls clad in Islamic dress and reciting koranic verses. Then reality dawned that the students, all girls, who were preparing for the West African School Certificate Examination, have indeed been abducted by the murderous criminal elements.

The fate of the students, some of whom were released in batches, remained a sore point, and a sad reference in the nation's war against terrorism and banditry. The situations tells volumes about the less than appropriate value for the lives of citizens, especially the vulnerable in the Nigerian society.

It is also a sad remembrance of the opportunistic nature of human beings, as the abduction of the girls was seen as an opportunity to unleash a 'revolution' against the then administration. The APC promised heaven and earth but unfortunately, instead of having all the girls released, 112 girls, whose fate have remained unknown, are still in the hands of the terrorists. Many other such brazen school abductions have taken place with very little or no active response by the Buhari's government. Buhari have instead chosen to negotiate and pay millions of naira to the terrorists each time such abductions occur which in effect may be the reason why the abductions have continued unabated.

For activists, the Chibok incidence became a strategic opportunity for a pedestal, in the end, those activists had no direction, no stated purpose and did not direct public opinion towards a change in the National psyche.

For the parents of the 112 students still in captivity, the yearly assurance by the government for the release of their children may have lost meaning, as they keep living with the trauma of not knowing the state of their children, whether they are alive or dead. Such an assurance as given by the Presidency surely makes no difference to them any longer. Nigerians have lost interest in the purported ability of a president who had achieved nothing but lie to the nation and the world at every opportunity

To share in the pains of the parents, 20 of whom have reportedly died, the world remembered the Chibok girls with renewed calls for their release. The speaker of the United States House of Representatives, Speaker Nancy Pelosi, who took to her verified Twitter handle, @SpeakerPelosi on Wednesday to call for the return of the girls.

Also, the Foreign Relations Committee of the US Senate, tweeting under the verified Twitter handle @SenateForeign, spared the girls their thought with this tweet: "After 7 years, it is still painful to reflect on the tragedy of the #ChibokGirls' abduction by #BokoHaram.

Congresswoman Lucille Roybat-Allard, also tweeted calls for the release of the kidnapped girls. To mark the seventh year anniversary of the abduction of the girls, international rights group, Amnesty International has some harsh words for the Federal Government, accusing it of not learning from the Chibok experience in protecting school children from attacks. The rights group said in a statement on Wednesday: "The Nigerian authorities' failure to protect school children from recent attacks clearly shows that no lessons have been learned from the Chibok tragedy. The authorities' only response to schoolchildren being targeted by insurgents and gunmen is to close schools, which is increasingly putting the right to education at risk. Whatever authorities are doing to tame this tide, it is not working."

As the world marked the anniversary of the abduction of the girls, a cross section of Nigerians are constantly reminded the government has over the years shown no commitment expected of a government whose citizens, especially girls, are with a violent group with no regard or respect for human lives. They are been fed with empty promises and verbal commitment without corresponding action.

At a meeting with Swiss President, Alain Berset in 2018, President Muhamadu Buhari had said that the Federal Government had put strategies in place to ensure the safe return of the girls. That his government was building on the past successes of securing the release of some of the Chibok girls and other abducted persons in the North-Eastern part of Nigeria.

He said: "we will continue to make the safe release of the remaining Chibok girls a priority and will welcome any kind of support from any quarters to make this happen." The reality on ground, however, is that instead of rescuing the 112 girls who are still in captivity, things have gone from bad to worse, as the nation has continued to witness embarrassing mass abduction of students and other Nigerians since the abduction of the Chibok girls, and most especially after giving his words in 2018.

Some recent mass abduction of students:

11th Friday December 2020, **300 students were kidnapped** by bandits at the Government Science Secondary School, Kankara, Katsina State.

17th February 2021, **27 students were abducted** by gunmen from their dormitory at the Government Science Secondary School in Kagara, Niger State.

26th February 26, 2021 – more than **300 students were abducted** when Bandits invaded the Government Girls Secondary School, Jangebe, Zamfara State.

11th March, 2021, **39 students were abducted** by bandits at the Federal College of Forestry Mechanization in Kaduna State. Only 5 were recently released.

Update on strike by medical doctors and medical professionals in Nigeria.

Abuja. The Federal Government has met with representatives of all the professional bodies and unions in the health sector over the issue of hazard allowance for health workers in government health establishments. According to the Government, it was in furtherance of the April 2020 Memorandum of Understanding (MOU) that it signed with the Health Workers in the wake of the COVID-19 pandemic. The Nigerian Medical Association (NMA), Joint Health Sector Unions (JOHESU), Pharmaceutical Association of Nigeria (PSN) made submissions to the meeting, amongst others. Ngige disclosed that the health workers proposed an increase to 65 years for medical officers and other health workers and 70 years for consultants. He said the meeting will reconvene in three weeks time for further deliberation.

The medical sojourn of Nigeria's President, Major General Muhammadu Buhari (rtd.), in London has entered its third week, fueling speculations of an extension of his medical sojourn in the United Kingdom yet the President's office has not issued an update on his London stay. It would be recalled that the Nigerian President supposedly travelled to London on March 30 for a "routine medical check-up", according to presidential spokesman, Femi Adesina. There have been no update as to his health and or the nature of his stay in London. Adesina in a statement titled, **'President Buhari Billed For Routine Medical Check-Up In London'** had said his principal "is due back in the country during the second week of April, 2021". But as at today (the third week of April), the President has not returned to the country, and the Presidency has not issued an update as to an extension of his London stay. However, Buhari's "short rest" at the Abuja House in London has been marred with the #HarassBuhariOutOfLondon protest organised by Reno Omokri, an ex-aide to former President Goodluck Jonathan. A counter-protest or a solidarity protest organised in support of the Nigerian president can be described as absurd drama.

While the #HarassBuhariOutOfLondon protesters want the President to return to the country and fix health care, among others, the solidarity protesters believe the President has a right to seek medical attention abroad even when medical professionals were being owed salaries and have downed tools in Nigeria. It is difficult sometimes to estimate where Nigerian problems lie, either with its ignorant leaders or its gullible minority who seem determined to destroy the nation instead of allowing peaceful coexistence or peaceful transition of the country into nation states.

This is not the first time the President will travel to London for medical purpose. According to PUNCH findings, between 2015 and 2019, Buhari spent a total of 404 days (a year and 39 days) travelling to 33 countries on four continents.

The country he visited the most was the United Kingdom where he spent 217 days mostly on health grounds and meetings of Commonwealth Heads of State and Government.

While in London this time around, resident doctors went on strike for at least 10 days. The strike, which commenced on April 1st was called off on April 10. Buhari has also been criticised for his medical trips abroad despite the huge amount allocated to the Aso Rock clinic annually. Buhari is away at a time when the Judiciary Staff Union of Nigeria has been on strike since April 6 over autonomy for the judiciary.

The President is also away at a time when different parts of the country boil with insecurity of rampaging fulani herdsnmen, killing indigenous people apparently with the tacit support of police and Army

News from the Diaspora

A Nigerian resident in Malaysia is facing deportation by the Malaysian Immigration service after he was notified of the intending deportation and was asked to prepare for it. SHAH ALAM: Nigerian national Simon Adavize Momoh, who has been detained at the Semenyih Immigration Depot for the last one month despite having paid his fine for a drink-driving offence, has been served a deportation order, his lawyer said today.

V Vemal Arasan said the order was emailed to Momoh's wife, Low Kar Hui, yesterday evening, asking her to prepare arrangements for his flight back to Nigeria.

He said that according to the deportation order, Momoh is deemed a prohibited immigrant pursuant to Section 8(3)(d)(i)(ii) of the Immigration Act. Vemal also told High Court judge Ab Karim Ab Rahman during a habeas corpus hearing seeking the release of Momoh that he had been unable to meet with his client at the detention centre yesterday. He said he needed to see Momoh to enable them prepare a proper submission, adding that the Attorney-General's Chambers (AGC) had agreed for him to liaise with his client. The Judge Karim set next Wednesday for a full hearing of his habeas corpus application. Vemal told reporters later there was no provision in the law to compel Momoh's wife to purchase a flight ticket for him to leave the country, adding that they may be writing an appeal to the government. Vemal filed the habeas corpus application on April 1, naming the Immigration Department, the Prisons Department and the home ministry as respondents. Momoh, who has been married to Low for the past eight years and has a valid visa, was arrested at a roadblock in Cheras in the early hours of March 15 on suspicion of drink-driving.

He plead guilty in court the same day, paid the RM12,000 fine, and his wife Low was told he would be released at 5pm. However, he has been detained at the Semenyih detention centre since then. Authorities previously denied access for Vemal and Low to meet Momoh, citing Covid-19 restrictions.

Religious Profiling: **Nigerian Army Killed 350 Christian Civilians In 10 Months And In Peacetime:** A gory tale of the unfolding genocide in Nigeria. Killings in the name of Religion. The International Society for Civil Liberties and Rule of Law (Intersociety) is deeply pained and saddened by indiscriminate massacring of defenseless civilians of Christian Faith by Nigerian Army. It says that Nigerian army now kill with reckless abandon and the uttermost impunity; it reports that in the past ten months from July 2020 to first week of April 2021, 350 defenseless Christian civilians, if not more, have been massacred by the Army in its supposedly peacetime internal security operations. The most disheartening of it all is that the defenseless victims, slain on the grounds of their religion and ethnicity, were summarily executed by soldiers in revenge for loss of their colleagues. That is to say that 'when criminal citizens attack and kill soldiers, the Army turns around and massacres defenseless civilians, especially Christian civilians in revenge and labels the slain victims as "hoodlums". Despite being paid and catered for on hourly and daily basis by Nigerians and their commonwealth to defend and protect defenseless citizens of the country and their properties, the reverse is now the case.

Religious Profiling And Hate Soldiering Are On Rampage: As part of its hate soldiering and religious profiling, the Army, from all indications, is deriving sadistic joy in turning its weapons of death against defenseless christian civilians at slightest or no provocation but rescinding same or looking blindly the other side when attacked by muslims in muslim areas. Following our recent investigative findings, it was found that the army lost at least 300 soldiers in 2020 and most of them were killed in the muslim held northeast and northwest by muslim insurgency groups and yet, heaven did not fall. The army also does little or nothing when muslim insurgency group like jihadist Fulani herdsmen and jihadist Fulani "bandits" attack and slaughter defenseless citizens especially christians. In the three months and ten days of this 2021, according to the Nigerian Security Weekly Tracker reports of the Council on Foreign Relations owned by John Campbell, a former US Ambassador to Nigeria, Nigerian army has lost a total of 70 soldiers, with 58 lost in Borno State alone, Nasarawa nine, Gusau three and so on (compared to about 25 in Benue, SS and SE); yet the attackers are still on the prowl and the communities where the attacks took place have not been wiped out or razed. Such muslim held communities including Damboa, Dikwa, Chibok, Maiduguri, Nasarawa, Gusau, Kukawa, Marte, Koya and Guzamala are till date inhabited and their houses, mosques and emir palaces intact.

On the contrary, a recent case in Akwa Ibom and Benue States. For losing 11 soldiers in Benue State, 100 defenseless christian civilians or more were massacred and dozens went missing, their dwelling houses and properties including the Palace of the respected traditional ruler of Agidi (Tyoor Unaha Koko) set on fire. In Akwa Ibom State (Essien-Udim LGA), for losing some police officers and others to criminal citizens, defenseless christian civilians numbering 30 or more were slaughtered by soldiers, their homes and properties burnt. Survivors were forced to flee and take refuge in a catholic church. According to facts emerging from Shangev-Tiev, Konshisha Local Government Area of Benue. Apart from the massacre of 100 or more, the Nigerian Army also 'bombed, razed and demolished farms, schools, hospitals and residences' belonging to over 15 rural christian communities of Bonta, Tse-Jembe, Tse-Anyom, Gbinde, Mbaakpur, Aku, Agidi, Gungul, Adoka, Guleya, Awajir, Shiliki, Achono and Ulam Communities" forcing thousands of natives to flee their homes till date.

Intersociety has also investigated and found that one of the major triggers of army targeted massacre of defenseless Christian civilian population are very slight or no provocation in Nigeria. Most especially if the Christian communities are within the territorial command of key military units under senior officers of Fulani-Hausa muslim extraction. On the other hand, it is also our finding that Christian Army commanders in Muslim held Northern part of the country are minutely insignificant in number. Where they are posted, they work under what appears to be "caliphate instructions". Take-over and control of key Army formations in Christian parts of the country by these Muslim officers is a deliberate policy of the present Government of Nigeria. This is responsible for disproportionate insecurity and safety of the affected Christian civilian population and their properties; thereby putting them not only in danger but also exposing them to attacks by jihadist Fulani Herdsmen, jihadist Fulani "bandits" and others.

How almost 350 Christian Civilians Were Massacred By Army In 10 Months

1. In Takum Taraba, 30 unarmed Christian civilians were killed by soldiers on 29th/30th June 2020 .

2. At Emene in Enugu, October at least 30 Christian civilians were killed.

3. On 20th Oct 2020, at least 20 mostly Christians were killed at Lekki in Lagos State and across the Southeast during EndSARS protests.

4. In the same Oct 2020, at least 30 defenseless Christian civilians were killed by soldiers in Enugu, Abia, Anambra, Imo and Ebonyi.

5. Between 21st Oct and mid Nov 2020, army massacred at least 102 Christian civilians in Obigbo and environs in Rivers State.

6. Between 14th and 22nd Jan 2021, army killed at least ten Christian civilians including six farmers in Orlu, Imo State.

7. On 5th April 2020, at least 30 Christian civilians were killed by soldiers in Essien-Udim, Akwa Ibom State.

8. On 6th to 7th April 2021, 100 Christian civilians or more were massacred by soldiers in Shangev-Tiev, Konshisha Local Government Area located in Benue State and dozens of others are still missing. These are just to cite but a few.

Campaign of Lies against Biafra

A lie is a falsehood, which before it was made, during and after the fact, remains false. It is known to the maker of it from the beginning that the assertion was not truth.

A half-truth also is a complete lie because it is, and was made with the express intention to deceive. Lies intends that the person who hears, will believe them and rely on them.

It is the human 'way of life' that every position we meet, we end up having people who would understand on either side of the divide. Let us use a movie as an example. Most people end up taking sides with the Hero yes, but regardless of anything any one may say, there are people who would understand and take the side of the villain, no matter how hideous the movie makers had portrayed such a character to be. That is exactly the truth of life. When the issue is of ethnic concern, truth may become irrelevant. A writer says, if a lie is believed for only one hour, it had done its damage. Lies moves faster than truths, like a raging fire, it is more appealing and gives leave for a myriad of amendments, adjustments and embellishments whereas truth has only one position.

In politics, there are men who deal in creating lies as a matter of their daily duty. Their every statement is a compendium of lies. Every speech, every communication are all complete falsehoods. They do consider the consequences of what they say, as the consquences are reasons for the lies. They do not even attempt to conceal their lies or to remember what lies they have told from one minute to the other; but to go on delivering, unrestrained arrays of lies from one press conference to another. Their only concern is that it be convenient for them to make any statement they chose, that the press repeat their words and that they should be free to make as many different falsehoods all the time. For them, your belief in what he had said or is saying, is completely irrelevant to him. Any attempt to revise any lie, being questioned on it, would just call up an entirely new set of lies, not withstanding if the new assertions are in anyway contradictory to what was said few moments ago.

Truth is that whether you believe him or not, makes no meaning to these types of politician. They derive their relevance by creating divisions among the people as a tool of continuity in public office. There is only one remedy to this type of politician.

Do not make any assumption based on what he had said, do not glorify it by repeating such lies unless you can categorically challenge the lie and never base any behavior or action on the lies.

We must pretend that the Liar had just mumbled unrecognizable words and report it as such. This will mean that the lies will not be repeated, will not be printed and will not be made available to those who would tend to believe the falsehood for any reason, at least from your own point of view. Some people would think that the liar is a success especially a political compulsive liar. Because he would draw crowds and have some people on his side, the thought may read like: "yes he is a liar but he did maintain his position and is a political success just by lying, he is not lying per se, he is using this method to push narratives favorable to 'us.'"

Mazi Nnamdi Kanu once said "if you pay Nigerian journalist well, they will report the goodness of satan." The press will show some youths admire a liar. Some people look at the glamour of the position held, not at the real carnage the person is causing in the society. Many **lies** are only inventions of the imagination of the maker and may spawn thousand versions of itself within a short period. Truth is slow and sustained but always suffers at the hand of lies. No one returns to redress lies or to chase after lies with the truth. In fact, many people who know or find out the truth eventually, will still remain silent when the lies are repeated in their presence later on.

True position is that at a point in time, people would not want to hear the truth. As the saying goes, "truth is painful." Who wants to hear what threatens their existence, their beliefs, or what makes them uncomfortable? They are bad news when lies are told.

Internet gives us all the possibility of putting our own information out, checking information, revising our thoughts and beliefs but also keeps information available forever. There remain those, whose position gives them a better platform to peddle information directly into the mainstream media while we labor in our different social media platforms to bring out the truth, that is a fact of life we must accept, however, while we struggle to educate our people and the world we cannot let lies and liars be a part of our strategy.

Why do people believe Lies?

Daniel Kahneman says that our human nature craves self-sustenance; it embarks on certain cognitive biases related to realization, enlightenment, knowledge and acceptance of facts in other to survive, reduce confusion, anxiety and to make life simple. In this way man tries to protect himself by application of certain concepts.

Confirmation bias: we only look for information that confirms our preconceived notions even when evidence to the contrary is there.

Denial effect: We deny the existence of information that challenges our established views, without any justification.

Overconfidence effect: Unwarranted confidence in our own knowledge become a tool we use to impress ourselves and others.

The Politician knows that if a lie is continued, people will assume it is the truth. Why wouldn't they believe? Because they will say "if it is not true, why not refute it?" Note also that refuting a statement or a narrative implies giving that narrative a full analysis. So a lie must first be presented as it was created by its author in other that it is characterized before another narrative is advanced to refute the implication either in toto or in part. The liar know this, therefore they also rely on those who wish to refute 'their' lies to further increase the effect of such falsehood in the society.

Why does politicians lie?

To create a shift in ideology with a false or damaging narrative. To attack an opposing viewpoint which show their irresponsibility or inactivity. To respond to indefensible claims against them. Downright dishonesty and use of institutionalized sectional dichotomy to cast an aspersion on political debate.

Response to lies told against Christians, Biafrans and IPOB

What then should we, who are at the receiving end of United Nation Organization lies and apathy to the genocide do? It is important to be resolute in the face of this emerging conflict. Never tell untruths or underestimate the resolve of the enemy. We should never become same as our enemies and detractors. We must ride on the advantage of being known for the truth; this may weaken our present circumstances but will always stand the test of time in the long-run. Biafra is forever, so we must remain resolute, committed and strong even as we engage in a serious war of independence. Our strength remains the fact that we are in our homeland they are the invaders.

Those who are against us have an overwhelming reason to push lies against us, but we have the singular truth of our position. Simply put is desire to live free, safe and sovereign in our homeland without being unnaturally taxed in life, resources or be subjugated. This struggle is between truth and falsehood and only one position is correct. We are on that truth.

Something about **truth** is that there are not much room for any other construction. For IPOB and Biafra the position is self-determination, it is as simple as that. The opposition can point to lies about every failed nation on earth, terrorism, bandits, herdsmen, criminality, constitution, bad leadership, restructuring, religion, cultural differences, resource mandate, every conceivable rhetoric but the central thing is that they are reeling out reasons against the truth: failure of the Nigerian State. Our position is only one: Biafra.

We cannot compromise on truth. It is our war plan, it is our organization and our battle plan too: Self-determination.

Now we get to the central problem we have. Initially IPOB and MNK the leader did not envisage an armed conflict. We have a good case and over the years, the evidence were increasingly pilling up. In the heart of every Biafran, we believed that the United Nations, and all other nations allied against Biafra in the 1960's would come to the realization that Biafra was not the aggressor at all.

Ojukwu after the war, from exile and after his return used every means at his disposal to reiterate this. He wrote his books and gave lectures. He told Igbo residents in every other part of Nigeria that the war was not yet over, but they would not listen attentively. Culturally we believed that truth will always win, that is who we are. But as the years went by, we realized, for the World, truth does not matter. The world need only to know "whose" resources are available for plunder. This realization started slowly and grew from strength to strength, today a Moses faces a Ramses and we know the whole story.

This day it is a world built on whichever road is easier to reconstruct. If the man with the gun shoots 200 people in the name of racism, we tell each other that he is mentally retarded; because we find it easier to offend his relatives than his entire race. Another man straps a bomb on himself and walks into a wedding feast proclaiming his faith. We will tell each other that religion has nothing to do with the massacre it was just a misguided fellow.

That is why Human Rights violations, corruption, false diplomacy and killings of every kind is going on simultaneously on every nation on earth today. From United States where racial killings of blacks have added a trend of rising attacks against Asians, the age-old Jew bashing, which need no introduction or reason. That was why China refused to be identified with a disease that originated there, yet any variant therefrom, is named accordingly (South African, United Kingdom, Brazil) variants. China know something the rest of the world refuses to say. Few days ago I watched Fauci in a panel being called all kinds of name for his lies and wickedness, no one brought the department heads or ministers who schemed to use a coronavirus pandemic to extort the world. We are still watching. Then every drug-producing nation was falling head over heels each other to make billions of dollars selling vaccines. That was why a special 'free' vaccine was being prepared for Africa. Men! Where went our mental faculties?

Now I come to the very reason I started this part of the essay, Mr. Peter Hawkins, UNICEF Nigerian representative to Nigeria gave an interview to United Nations Radio presenter where he stated:

"SUCH INCIDENTS HAVE BECOME A WAY OF LIFE TO MANY NIGERIANS..."

This statement above alone has exactly described what he, personally and the entire UNITED NATION as an organization, think about Nigeria. This struggle to extricate ourselves from an artificial contraption of Britain is stifling us all and promises to kill all of us in the process with the blessing of the silent world.

A way of life, means the course of conduct, a normal method of living/doing things, a usual phenomenon, been accepted as common, just, acceptable and proper.

Mr. Hawkins did not even attempt to put a negative word in other to smoothen his hatred of us. He is telling the world in his capacity as the UNICEF personality living and representing the world here that: "Kidnapping of school children is a normal thing in Nigeria, that it is and have been the norm, it is their way of life."

To buttress his point, he went on to praise the government for ATTEMPT to negotiate with terrorists, bandits and killers. By this, comfortably refusing the fact that Nigerian military were positioned to kill, rape, terrorize and maim innocent unarmed Biafrans in southern Nigeria whereas the terrorists, bandits and killer herdsmen are rampaging in the northern Nigeria, freely without security challenge from the national armed forces.

Then he began to lecture the world "Happily" that the situation now had even improved from what it was in 2015 and 2016.

I am terribly outraged, he was planted, he was told what to say, he is under remote. Incidentally just a day prior, a radio station interviewer had sought to get Aisha Yesufu to praise the government for paying ransom but she was outraged, screaming HOLY MURDER!

Mr. Hawkins if you enter "Facebook" please search: KIDNAPPED VICTIMS REPORTS IN NIGERIA. You will realize how mistaken you are. Kidnapping had never been acceptable to us, it is not normal too. Aisha's reply to the Journalist was: "When you have been kidnapped and ransomed by the government, then I will praise the government for the rescue". One moment I will gladly give Aisha a resounding applause, being in opposition to her on the issue of her stand on our fight for self-determination. I will not make that same prayer for you because of obvious reasons, however I call on you to render an apology to the INDEGENOUS PEOPLES of the Nigerian contraption against whom your assault was targeted.

We are human, we know the difference between good and bad, we have been living free and happy before the arrival of colonialism, we love, we smile, we dance, we quarrel, we make up, we are a normal people who have produced all manner of talent for ourselves and for the entire world. We know we are being assaulted by you and the organization you represent because of natural resources within our lands. We have decided to stand up, to live, not exist on the fringes of society. If you live in Nigeria, you know that we do not carry or even own guns and other explosive weapons. So how is kidnapping for ransom a WAY OF LIFE IN NIGERIA? It is statements like this, make people scared when they see us on the streets of Europe. Kidnapping, killings, rape, etc. are 'their' way of life, you said? That is why all our appeals against the assault on the indigenous people have not been given the correct attention by the United Nations. You and people like you always give a false report back to your headquarters contradicting whatever is happening on the grounds in the country.

Now back to us my brothers and sisters! Let no one tell you a lie, we cannot easily achieve self-determination with these type of forces amassed against us. We have the truth and that is all we need the rest is to follow the leadership of our struggle and find the future for ourselves. Truth alone will get us just so far, the rest is a determined and formidable decision we must make when the time comes to fight with all we can muster. Mazi Nnamdi Kanu and Mazi Simon Ekpa have all it takes to lead us to the second mile. We must be that **Igurube** (**chikota ukwu o gbaka ite**) jointly to lean on each other join our legs and collectively deliver a kick that will break the pot.

Colonial wars for Biafra

The Dahomey kingdom which was in the present day Benin was a very powerful Kingdom, but finally all the Kingdoms of west African fell to the Europeans. Sometimes this was achieved by war or genocide, at other times through cunning, outright falsehood and or by trickery. The natives would welcome their guests but the same guests would turn to monsters even as they looked on.

Dahomey's last King, King Shark fought French forces to a bitter end. At his peak he was said to have commanded 150,000 men and 5,000 all women fighters known as the Amazons. Today he is still one African leader who never submitted to Europeans and fought for his people to the end.

The Igbo homeland is a large forested hinterland in South eastern Nigeria where the people had no centralized government. Every village of about 5 kilometer square miles or more, were entirely independent. They govern themselves, regulate themselves in every way and does not concern themselves with every other areas near or far away to them. All Biafran communities or villages and clans were related to each other through marriages, shared festivals, market, seasonal celebrations and family ties running through thousands of years. So much so that one clan can mediate for its neighbor with another distant clan, if they can find a link through ancestry or marriage.

Blood relationship limits marriageability in Briafran clans. Therefore, marriage is very important method of linking villages together. Presently in today's Biafra, cultural marriages where a man 'Obi', from village 'Uzu' desiring to marry a girl 'Ngozi' from village 'Imo'. Would search in Imo village for someone related by blood to anyone from Uzu village. It does not matter how distant the relationship is, a male member of that family will be his go-between in the marriage rites of Obi to Ngozi. So though Igbo villages are independent of each other, they are technically related to one another. They share language dialectics, markets, religious and cultural ceremonies and they depend on each other as any nation on earth would depend on others for trade, defense, sports, health, research and educational exchanges.

Biafra villages were therefore almost impossible to subjugate as a whole. The British empire had to fight running battles one community after another and as they recorded gains, many villages regrouped and relaunched another war repeatedly against colonialism.

The colonial wars for Biafra-land started when the British launched an attack against Opobo and other coastal villages with the aim of controlling the trade in Oil palm and other products. Igbo wisdom had through the ages discovered the use of religion to enforce law and order in the life of the society. Therefore the priestly class held the secret of the traditional religion; using edicts supposedly from divination of the Gods to enforce good societal norms and practices. This wisdom guided by a system of secrecy is enforced by threat to life, achieved against the guilty party in claiming that the will of God had been achieved. The priests of the different Gods each held different secrets related to use of native healing herbs for the treatment of diseases, wound care, bone setting, antidote to snake venom, among others. Native priests hold both temporal and spiritual powers, they vary in their character and skills. As stated above poison was an essential part of their trade so by declaring the wrath of God on dissents they could craftly poison such an opposition and declare that God had decided. They held the peoples trust therefore. People consulted the Arochukwu God and accepted the dictation of the God and their priests, this was not acceptable to the British.

However you look at ancient Biafra land, our Gods and our system made us who we are, we had pride and we had respect for each other borne out of pure knowledge and wisdom. We honored and respected hard work, we honored and exalted feats of human achievement in the arts, music, and dance. We respected people for special talents in healing, carving, sculpture, smithing, mining and fearlessness in traveling to strange lands and or learning new things for the motherland.

We sat around to negotiate our existence and held each man accountable to their deeds. Arochukwu refused to give up their independence.

The Arochukwu confederacy, a group of clans that have either Aro-indigenes or are protected by the Aro clan fought the British onslaught. It was a war for the control of trade in Biafra land. The Britain could not stomach repeated disruption of their trading parties by Aro warriors. This descended into a war on all Igbo towns and villages. It is recorded that tens and thousands of Biafrans were killed in the war from 1901 to 1902.

Ekumeku uprising is another alliance of Igbo communities against Britain. The reason given in Bitish parliament was to control trade and enforce the ban on slave trade, but it was also a reprisal for the treatment of the British explorers. Lander brothers had died at the hands of Anioma nation, when they were tracing the source of the Niger. Lander brothers could not explain satisfactorily to the natives why they were crossing through their territories. We know today that Anioma communities were correct. Those explorers were actually spies and should have been treated as such. They opened the way for the rape and destruction of our cultures with heir exploratory journeys. So the British found out over a 31-year war experience. Ekumeku introduced them to Biafra land.

In 1880 The Royal Niger company invaded Atani and there was the legendary genocide described in Chinua Achebe's book 'Things fall apart'.

In 1897, Onicha-ado was bombarded, Ibusa followed, then Ibuza counter attacked. A Missionary father Zappa reported repeated reinforcements of Ibuza forces when the British thought the natives would surrender. Because of the need for soldiers, the British conscripted soldiers from Hausa nations and launched major attacks killing everything that moves human or animal alike. Farms, villages, forests were sacked as they burnt down and killed everyone to achieve their aim. Remember Britain then was a nation, supposedly opposed to slave trade but was then committing genocide on Biafran nations in the name of enforcing ban on slave trade.

The Owa battle was so brutal that leutenant Moorhouse had to defend himself on why he sustained casualties. In that battle, British soldiers used 4 connaught rangers, 2.95 artillery and Bazooka cannons, among other weapons. Captain Crewe was killed in this said battle.

Ogwashi-uku war began in 1909 with a mandate to the British forces to kill everyone on their way. 34 British soldiers were killed and countless native Hausa soldiers died including Captain H. C. Chapman. It was here they realized native fighters were coming from neighboring communities to fight whenever the battle moves from a conquered community to another community.

British war tactics included forced seizure of food stuff, assault on females and indiscriminate killings even of captured Ekumeku warriors.

I would agree we were beaten from the word go, because the British empire had overwhelming experience, resources and colonies from where their power could flow-in, time and again. We had only our few native swords, bows and arrows but we did learn fast. As one village fell the next geared up to war. Britian fought community after community, the Olokoro clan followed, then Uzuakoli in Bende, the Akwette communities took up arms. The Onitsha expedition followed by 1905, the Ezza war, the Ovorro War, Nuyna war, Onicha and Ahiara battles. 1907 the Isuikwuato war, the Urualla war, the Etche war, the Ntarakpu and the Isiagu wars in succession one after the other. Biafran villages never gave up.

The major problem for Britain was that many battle fronts regrouped and relaunched an attack against British forces, sometimes mere days or weeks after being defeated. It was here, it was there. The war seemed to be the first "war without end" until the frustrated British became downright dirty. They killed for the pleasure of it, they begun to dehumanize, assault, rape and humiliate captured elders in front of the villages then summarily execute captives.

Many British soldiers were decorated for their participation in those wars of annihilation. William Heneker commanded Uli and Ishan expedition, March 1901, the Ibeku -Olokoro operation and the Afikpo operations.

John Mackenzie received a brevet promotion to Major in 1902

Archibald Hayes Macdonald received medals of honor for Ibeku expedition, Ibeku - Olokoro expedition, Mkpani expedition and Obokum expeditions.

The motivation for the colonial assaults on the new worlds was pure displacement of native cultures and supplanting these nations. So young men of Europe were well motivated, well armed against native people who had only sticks and matchets to defend themselves but then we did defend ourselves.

Effective colonization launched the period of rape and plunder of the resources of Biafra. Major efforts at colonization began with the churches. The colonial administration brought missionaries in the name of Christianity. They provided education and healthcare in exchange for the people's way of life. Much like Bishop Desmond Tutu's famous statement: 'They came holding the bible and said let us pray, by the time we opened our eyes, Biafra was holding the bible and Britain was in possession of our lands.

Our names were rejected,

Our religion was rejected

The color of our skin became the color of a non existent devil

Linguists coined words like black-mail, black-list, black-market et cetera

Every unfortunate circumstance become depicted as black

Victory and success becomes white

Ghosts we were told are black while angels become white

The dehumanization process is still continuing even as we speak.

The assaults of so many hundreds of years have confused and distracted many of our people so much that we need a concerted period of another re-education to attempt to make our people regain their dignity and pride. Today the major problem is from within our hearts. Many Biafrans still hold tenaciously to the tutelage of subjugation, which will take generations to change.

Movies depicting ghosts, mummies, witches and wizards, orcs, dwarfs and every other villain and evil as black. By comparison elves, angels, and every other heroic characters are white. I know someone would say this assertion is an over simplification of the matter, but this is exactly the issue at stake, something as mundane as everyday thoughts and reasoning has an overwhelming influence on our person, our actions and our behavior. We must completely overturn this rhetoric from the smallest fact to major issues. We must use truth and facts. We must use historic circumstances facts and figures to educate each other.

Let us look at the exact wording of a treaty supposedly entered into by a king

"I, Docemo, do with the consent and advise of my Council, give, transfer, and by these **presents** grant and confirm unto the Queen of Great Britain, her heirs and successors for ever, the Port and

Island of Lagos, with all the rights, profits, territories and appurtenances whatsoever thereunto belonging...freely, fully, entirely and absolutely...."

I will leave the analysis of the above document to you.

The formation of international institutions in the twentieth century occurs under a scenario marked by the rule of colonialism and imperialism. Thus, instead of reducing inequalities in the world system, international institutions reproduced a prevalent logic of material and subjective discrimination based on a colonialist ideology marked by violence, which is communicated in a certain way so that it can justify its importance and legitimacy. Colonial violence is perpetuated under a form of symbolic violence manifested in the language that imposes a universal meaning. Or systemic violence that manifests itself in the 'perfect' functioning of the world economic and political system as the ultimate form of development. One of the perverse and subtle dimensions of this violence is observed in the emergence of the International Environmental Law in terms of meta-narratives that exclude minorities and perceptions other than the ones propagated by international institutions. The main objective of this article is to identify the dynamics in the formation of environmental treaties leading to standard results of discursive practices that feed the process of dependence and legitimization marked by colonial ruling and structural violence. The methodological approach relies on the critical theory, tenets to expose the non-emancipatory features of current International Environmental Law. For that matter, this article applies the socio-legal approach to environmental treaties that consists of the analysis of text (law), subtext (the moral aspects of the law – deep or implicit meanings), and context (the undeniable connection between law and reality) in the search of empirical evidence.

Britain is fond of pitting race against race all through the years of colonialism. So through several decades and generations, lack of trust would remain among indigenous people, maybe forever.

You must appreciate that when a people are intrinsically evil, everything they think and do automatically tends to be evil. We must know and accept this very fact in other to understand why it seems Europe appear not to notice the decadence in Nigeria. Their masses know and see, they are the people we should appeal to for to join our protests and speak for us. The policies of leadership seeks only selfish interests and so the availability of Biafran resources in Nigeria are all these nations would see, not the sufferings or injustices metted out against Biafrans. Individually however we could appeal to and get necessary support to ginger our freedom. However, our primary engagement is to the powers that be, even though we know what response we are expecting. Any fight for freedom is a protracted war, being determined and resolute is a must, wisdom and precision is another important fact because Nigeria would not bat an eye to eliminate our leaders. United Kingdom have been doing so for ages and they would continue if we let down our guard.

Carnage grow fingers

Today in “Biri Kam Biri,” we talk about enlightenment and education and wisdom and how they can be confusing. If you assume that one is superior to the other, if you are made to accept that education can give you ‘everything’ in life. ***Obu na aguba adighi nko, ka obu n’okpuisi amaghi akpu,*** (this translates to: In the hands of a paralytic, the sharpest sword is harmless, but in the hands of a fool the dullest sword is extremely dangerous).

I am telling you that our work is to write and write and educate our people. Education is absolutely empowering and you can see the increasing resistance to bad government of Nigeria. It is not yet over, we have to keep showing our people what we all need to know, in other to better our lots. Keep writing people, we have to forget the mainstream media. They are paid to hide truth and deceive people with lies. The silence of BBC and CNN and other international media houses constitute falsehood and denial of the genocidal carnage going on in Nigeria. A foreign current affairs analyst on Simon Ekpa's programme had said that he does not think that our stories are being heard all over the world. Regardless of what we think about his take on the matter, we should go on to remove that excuse from the United Nation and from all other nations on earth by flooding the social media with information and by creating as many news, radio and television stations too. Write and write and write. Share truth when you see it especially video evidences. Be ready with your phones to record and send in online. Only our efforts can change our destinies. Yes, the successes may seem little now but do not worry, time will vindicate the truth. If we now know the difference from politics and the demands of governance. We cannot allow our collective destinies to become politics. We need to take control of ourselves for good governance, we do not need politics.

You know some people are still justifying their actions during the last two general elections in Nigeria by claiming that time was to blame. Well a mistake is a mistake and the best thing we can do is to accept responsibility and determine not to fall for it again. Let me tell you; the situation in 1819; is just as different from 2019 because of the difference in persons facing issues on those specific dates. If one had decided to make a false decision granting the knowledge available at the time in 1819; if you bring him to 2019 and give him the knowledge available in 2019 he would still make a bad decision. It is as simple as that. If you had voted for Buhari in 2015 well of cos 98% of Igbo did not vote him (remember 97% and 5%, saga) there is a chance you can redeem yourself by becoming part of the present solution. There is no other time for recalling bad leadership. If you called it a mistake in 2015 what happened in 2019. Well, that is why we have individual autonomy, please be clear on this: Life is going on, ethnicity or best candidates cannot wait for our future if you know what I mean. It is your choice not mistake. Let us not try at all. How is it that we have to try, try, try, what trying is that? With our time and collective destinies? How many persons have tried to cut their legs with a hoe; yes we know the knife cuts, but try with a hoe or try with a chisel, no! no! no! try to cut your leg with a log of wood. You know it is blunt but yes, let us try it. Have you tried running into a tree? Yes if the car drives and hits a tree it will crash. What if I just run into a tree, or let us roll into the ocean not dive. They are two different things. Not dive, let us try rolling and see if the ocean will still drown us. So why would you try giving the entire Nigeria into the hands of someone whose brother is determined to kill everyone, who has no dreams, no ideas, empathy or even our collective interests at heart. Tell me the difference between half a dozen and six. Our mumu still remain.

Why do you think that Nigeria keeps failing at everything, even some years ago when we had the best dream team in the world, issues of remuneration comes to fore because, half of them were Biafrans. Do you not yet realize that the bane of Nigeria is Institutionalized ethnic intolerance? We must put in sub-standard staff as a matter of law even though it would lead to the collapse of the industry. Are we actually sane? Then let Biafra lead Biafra, Oduduwa, Arewa and other nations go their separate ways, and being unburdened by the weight of tribalism bring their best brains, talents and men to administration and governance of their nations. This would be good for its peoples and the world in general.

I know that Muhamadu Buhari, have made us all realize the importance of education. There is nothing more important than giving or getting the best education possible, whether it is through formal or informal systems. We can all see what we have done to ourselves. But let me tell you that Northern Nigeria will never get it no matter how it is decorated or presented. Because the policy of ethnicity prevents their youths from learning, therefore there is no meeting point between Arewa and Biafra.

We have systems and processes in life, even when we know that there are exception to every rule. We live in the same country, we buy from the same market, we have families and friends who are in the same country. We know there are graduates of English language who are not proficient in English. In fact, we know sometimes, natural wisdom can eclipse intelligence. But, these and other related issues are incidental, not the norm. No matter how intelligent a young man of thirty can be, there is a greater wisdom in a wizened old man of 70. That is predicated on the older man being sane, properly, traditionally educated and having lived a meaningful life through which he has acquired the wisdom accruing due to age. However, in terms of those systems and processes, in terms of administrative efficiency, in terms of the zeal to meet challenges and the strength to carry out pledges, inspire confidence and engage the development of the present. A youth at forty to forty five would far out-perform his grand-Father. Referring to a youth at 45, I have in my mind a careful controlled and intelligent man driven by the passion to make a statement in the lives of his people. A man of compassion and wisdom who feels the plight of his generation. That is Mazi Nnamdi Kalu and Mazi Simon Ekpa and their leadership. In whatever things we are doing, we move holding onto the truth of the situation. Believing that the exception can also be true, is not correct. That is why it is known as an exception and not the basis for decision making.

We in Biafra have this assertions of: "does he feed me?" Implying that our personal ability to cater for ourselves is evidence we do not need a lawyer, we do not need a doctor, we do not need an engineer, we do not need a teacher, and so on. What a catastrophic assumption. But you can see where it is keeping us today. There is a reason the four walls of the school, would instill greater wisdom not only knowledge on a person who had been there, than one who dropped out or never went in. Degrees and certificates are awarded based on "having successfully passed and allowed the institution to pass through…." The arguments that some other engineer cannot repair a car is only true for lack of practical experience. Put him to work and see. For he learnt the principles with minimal practical experience. But the car works on principles only: Intake – compression – power - exhaust; when he finally get to work, the pieces would fall in place simple. There is no comparison at all; because you would compare the best in the two arms of learning. You cannot compare a "let my people go" graduate of mechanical engineering, with an excellent road side mechanic. Therefore, let us accept that we made a colossal wrong choice from the beginning. I tell you in truth, the conditions, the successes, the failures, the development and future of a people lies in their hands only" if we keep covering our faces like the proverbial Ostrich to bury our heads in the sands, our problems will forever be our problems. Until we decide, enough is enough that is when our mumu would do. I am not interested in how many people are falsely empowered, but in empowering the entire Biafra nation with a responsible sovereign state of its own. We need more wisdom to be freely given out, to educate our people and let them realize it cannot be work as usual. The Army, the police, other security operatives of Biafran extraction count your teeth with your tongue, for if you continue to prop up a dead kingdom, your own destiny would be blighted forever.

Sometimes our leaders are not only short sighted but down right blind. There is nothing you can say to convince them. My present mental disposition is to fight my cause to the best of my abilities and let history tell it all. Mazi Nnamdi Kalu, is entirely correct right now and given Nigeria as it is structured he would have been correct in 1971 as well as would be in 2069 in the future. Archbishop Obinna when he was a young priest moderated a leadership retreat for National Federation of Catholic Students held at Alvan Ikoku. I attended that conference as a representative of my College then. The highlight of that three days retreat, was the struggles by the Catholics in Kaura Namoda polytechnic 1988/1989. At the time of the conference the problem was still on going. Whether a church would be built and how high would the roof and a cross on top of it be. This had led to killings and closure of the school, have resulted in religious crisis in the town and across all the northern states in the country. Till this day, no politician has been able to address religious intolerance. I have not mentioned resource control, good governance, infrastructural development, education and the issue of correct states, I have not mentioned health care industry and the metal ceiling placed on every Igbo man. I remember some few months ago a delegate of the IPOB met with Archbishop Arinze asking for his support. Our brother, Archbishop asked them to form a political party and fight for elections. There is a fundamental question every of these learned men are cleverly trying to sidestep. Is Nigeria structured to give its citizens justice and Peace? Please my spiritual father Archbishop Arinze, put a few munites call to Archbishop Kuka and have a chat with him. Try to contact Obadiah Mailafia for a private meditation together. Talk to Governors Aminu Bello Masari and Kashim Shettima. The case of TY Danjuma and Gowon, my father I guess you need to educate me on that but they all point to one direction and the cause of insecurity in this fake nation. I have the utmost respect for you intellectually, spiritually you are my father too. But in the matter of Igbo self determination please I beg to disagree WE ARE CORRECT THIS TIME, My Lord. A word of wisdom is important here: "odughu ife imere ka obi di onye iro mma" (there is nothing you will do to appease someone who hates you) even if you die, the enemy will still be angry that you are not alive, so he can see and enjoy your suffering. IPOB need your support Archbishop, look critically on the matter at hand from every angle, there are no short fixes, who will rise up for the people if not us, who?

Now to the entire world starring with unseeing eyes at the genocide in Nigeria against Biafra, I am disappointed with you failure once again; the same way the world abandoned the Tamils of Sri Lanka, is the same way they are treating the Syrians, Yemenis and Biafrans. It has nothing to do with religion and race. The world only responds to "interests". If there are sufficient interests, then sorry if you happen to fall into the opposite site to those INTERESTS. It does not bother the United Nations, well UN is presently engaged with the origin of the Coronavirus. Same thing happening in Yemen. This gives me a lot of reasons to doubt the whole United Nations hullabaloo and rhetoric about Palestine. So the Syrians, the Yemenis, Christians and Biafrans in Nigeria are less human? No not at all. They have shared the important resources of these nations. So sorry those people you are mentioning Iwunna, just happen to be on the other side of the divide.

Buhari, congratulations, you said it 'the dog and the baboon will all be soaked in blood!' You are correct, only this time around you may not come out unscathed we read the times and we are determined. I did not get who or what was said in the case of the Yemenis, Libyans and all others. Please share if you did. Once we are able to say it as it is, our work is done. But we must keep talking, so that those who have ears may hear, as for the understanding thereof; special divine intervention is not necessary all that is needed: arms and willingness to use it. They are teaching the next generation of war mongers how it is done.

Even our Pope Francis know it, unless we fight back, and unless we fight back on time and do so with a more determined sense of purpose, with greater ferocity than them, we shall not survive their onslaught. Day one, today ten death recorded. Day two, next day, 12 murders recorded. Do we actually think the numbers will stop or increase? Official government tally is around 30,000 murdered with tens of millions displaced as at March, 2022. Are we learning to count? Do we not realize that this is GENOCIDE? When will this counting exercise be tallied? What total are we looking for? At what number do we determine it? Yes, may I ask if they are counting material and psychological losses too? Some middle belt peoples will never be the same again while we are doing this addition exercise. Gowon and T.Y. Danjuma, been traumatized to the highest level (two Nigerian Generals who commanded and processed the genocide against Biafra in 1966 to 1970 genocide) for good measure, everyone must have a taste of this evil. The crux of the matter today is to halt a genocide that is happening right now. Being politically correct would lead to another world war. Call a spade a spade and nothing else. Do not forget that Donald Trump was able to win elections because he had the courage to say what needed to be said, we need world leaders who can do that and be sane enough to know the difference between Xenophobia and tacit support of evil in the name of political correctness. Nigerian government is responsible for what is happening not Boko Haram, not bandits, not herdsmen who are all friends and partners with the government. Nigerian government is guilty of carrying out a covert operation to exterminate a section of it's own people. If this is not true what else is. I will say it as an ancient Igbo proverb had: ***obu nani osisi g'anu n'aga egbu ya kwuru nga ono***, (only a tree would stand where it is, and do nothing after hearing it would be cut down).

Things happen at their appointed times. We have a lifetime to live and we must not plan for today alone. We should plan for that lifetime, even as we are not aware when it starts or when it may end. But then as much of it as we are aware of, we must plan to the extent providence allows us to, that is our lifetime.

Best laid out plans will fail, plans made without a thought to our mortality will fail too. The only real plan that would serve its purpose within the ambit of our liveable lifetime, is a plan, which is made to survive to the point of our exit but also affords our next of kin a leeway into their own next step. We talk and talk but if we have no solutions to the problems and or if we offer no avenues into a possible solution, then what is the importance of our lectures? So I think we should look at our problems from a different perspective. Listen to the clamoring in Syria answered with gunfire, missiles and bombardment, we see a group of nations flexing their muscles there also, from America to Russia and many in between. To the tears of the Yemenis and the response with gunfire, missiles and bombardment. Congo, Iraq, Libya and Somalia have not yet stabilized from the trauma of 1990's and early 2000's assaults. Now we can be sure that nations and not only people go through a long time of PTSD following a radical period of upheaval; yet many regions are not learning from the trauma of others. In fact, the thirst for conflict seems to be ingrained in our human DNA. Such that MAN courts strife, seeks it out, listens in the silence of peace for the drums of war; which are strummed repeatedly by people for whom the daily laughter of children and the natural rhythms of native life is ANATHEMA. People who do nothing but crave for the resources of their neighbors, those that derive pleasure from the pains and pangs of destruction. Who see progress only when it walks on home streets. THEY WILL NEVER HAVE IT. Look carefully my friend, you can see the future theatres of conflict in Nigeria, the war mongers are keeping it on hold so that they may take time to utterly destroy the present houses of conflict. Then they would carry their war machines down to Nigeria. But, why do we listen to the dogs of war, why do we dance to the call of the hounds when they roar in the dead of nights? We should wage peace when war is proclaimed to us from the blood stained pulpits of the weapon factories. We should reach out with conditions for an acceptable settlement before even the arrival of the evil dancers. How should we do this?

If Nigeria and Cameroon announce today the passage of laws which puts into play, a period for referendum and subsequent creation of Biafra, Oduduwa and Arewa nations amongst others for Nigeria and Ambazonia for Cameroon. Will our collective DNA automatically denature itself? Catalonia on one hand and in many other places too, like the Kurds etc. Who told you that your greatness and success and stability as a nation and a people, is dependent on being bound to a people and an area that would not assimilate with you. Nature has immiscible substances so also does it have people who cannot or would not assimilate with you. Why do you think your existence is threatened by the freedom and possible success or failure of another. I dare to say Malaysia unitarily freed Singapore in the 1960's barely 5 years into single union nationhood. Today, both countries have survived and do consider each other brothers more than you can imagine. Millions of Singaporeans and Malaysians cross the causeway each day. I know if any of this two nations is radically threatened from outside; each would stand shoulder to shoulder to support the other. They did not fire, have not fired a single bullet to achieve what they have today, so why does the Hausa/Fulani assume that without the oil from the bight of Biafra they would cease to exist. Why wouldn't the Kurds, the Ambazonians, the Houthis, the Syrians, Taiwan or Hong Kong walk free as they please. Because, we humans have evil bottled up in us, to seek to destabilize our near neighbors defined by racial or ethnic differences. Because we seek to enslave others even if it means holding ourselves hostage. History will never stop to teach us its truth. The down trodden have never really accepted defeat. If there is a will, a way would show itself. In the meantime let the evil drummers keep up their destructive work, someday a Cyrus would rise up as King and HE would declare, without a referendum and the war machine, "Let the peoples return to their natural homelands and be unto themselves a nation in peace". The stronger powers must not call the weaker to a conference, for in the heart of every man is embodied a spiritual conscience to discern every fact and every situation and every circumstances amongst his people. Let go of dishonest rhetoric, irresponsible hullabaloo, useless conditions and standards. Only the truth shall set you free. No amount of force can buy you loyalty, it took about 400 years but where are American slave descendants today, freedom must be attained...

I just lost my will to continue this article again. Someone said that Fela's songs in the 1970's are still issues on board today. Another Gani Fawehimi's article from the 1980's seems to have been written yesterday, to make matters worse, the names of a few current leaders of the people were in that very article. The Newswatch magazines and old daily newspapers should be reprinted from 1987, they are all current affairs of today's 2020/21 except for the pandemic. So I have lost my zeal to speak or even write or contend the lack of progress.

The only thing that we seem to have kept abreast of other nations or even surpassed many others are the spate of killings, by murderous fulani herdsmen, kidnapping by gangs of abandoned youths (manpower that should have been trained to be meaningfully engaged in the job of nation building). We have wanton desecration of the principles of religion through irresponsible use of oratory and deceit. The level of destructive tendencies in the country today exceeds some war zones elsewhere in the world. Where are the stadiums to enable sports development and engagement of our youth in that aspect of human endeavor but we have hundreds of churches some church buildings seat hundreds of thousands of worshippers. Where are the companies and manufacturing concerns, do we have healthy SME's and enabling strategies and government industrial reserve areas? To kick start local investments and encourage international investors too, but we have an ever increasing pool of schools, universities, polytechnics, colleges of education that are seasonally turning out thousands of graduates yearly, and we have millions of almajiri beggars roaming the northern states. Hunting grounds for terrorists and bandits for sure.

Well as I stated above I have lost interest to continue this write up. I do not wish to be another voice that will rise, live and die at old age with the system not even acknowledging the words of the masters. I prefer to revisit those masters of whom I spoke about and recycle their words and speeches, those are still as vividly current today as when they were uttered 30 to 40 years ago....

I leave you with this poem:

Listen to the carnage grow fingers

Follow the screams where they lead

The journey of old had been for wealth

Today new roads are paved in blood

Last years harvest ripe and heavy as gold

This age only count in tears and graves

Listen to the screams describing horror
Follow the jingles that celebrates the act
Like in the laughter of Nero at the Arena
Incredulous that blood can lead to pain
Through the monocles let us draw nearer
Maybe this journey needs some faith

The wailers bleed, the terrible costs
At the open gates of heaven they lie
Abel in protest for his brother's wrath
When the race begun we cannot tell
Now too we become unwilling spectators
To the movement and the journey of blood

The Songs and dances at Ebo, rythms of lore
Immerses the earth in eternal courage
Rattles the tree where my birth-links hung
My foot cannot remain still, my body awakes
Today, swords and evil hearts chill my blood
As the voice of Dede warns of evil times

All over the land, the planet is festering
Men search the moons and mars for life

But destroy with abandon this earth

East and West there is no home

When we contrive to lay waste this earth

The only one which is given for mankind.

The lies of the global village

When I was younger, it was easier for me to let it be, when things go against me regardless of what was correct. Really, the church trained me like, drilling into us that "God knows the truth" is a much more important fact than fighting for your right. That is a very wrong way of training a child, because it leads to many sad times. People grow up believing they can offload their sadness or problems on us Christians. Well, in the times we live in, truth suffers. You read the newspapers, you listen to the radio, and watch television. May I ask how you feel as a Biafran?

You as the opinion leader, as a teacher and as a professional in your field of endeavor or just the man on the street. How do you feel when you hear the state governors spend thirty minutes on air lying to himself and to us all?

How do you feel when Lai Mohammed drops a few comments, when the villagers are put to confusion looking for where to get some clarity? My little analogy goes like this, these groups at the newspaper stands arguing about whatever nonsense the government have said or not said. They fight among themselves, half on the different sides of opinions. That was before Mazi Nnamdi Kalu came along and took the bulls by the horns. Now we realize Nigeria is entirely without a leader for the simple reason that our so called leaders are not inspiring by any standard. There are no programs for our day to day progress as a nation in the short or long term. Their promises are fake, their intentions are different from their spoken words. Their tomorrow does not have you or me written there in. We exist just to be used and discarded. I am calling you to witness this today, because our common 'in-action' is not propping up this status quo; it is legitimizing it. We must refuse vehemently from carrying weights that were not destined for us. The state of affairs of a people, a community, a state or a nation is exactly how they want it to be. Prove me wrong! Mazi Nnamdi Kalu has set the pace and we must all support him to change our sorry state of affairs right now. Thank God there is a general consensus all over Nigeria today as the education has borne good fruits. We must build on this success as a people regardless of the silence and insensitivity of the United Nations oganization to the genocide going on in Nigeria.

Very many years ago, Ted Turner floated the idea of the global village while he was building the CNN. It worked as he anticipated, after all, the military had been using satellites for many years spying on each other and selectively picking out their enemies at will. I will not digress here one bit. We can remember when satellites first filled the skies and countries stumbled over each other to launch theirs or to key into other country's satellites. Tell me my brother and sister, when the five super powers made peace as much as to jointly own the international space center. Now an American astronaut, a Russian cosmonaut, a french space engineer, a British mathematician, a south African tourist, a German surgeon and an Arab billionaire can all share the same living space aboard the International Space Center. Did we fail to identify the exact smoment in this journey of discovery when racism, religion, language, color and nationality disappeared. You still want me to believe that we are all different? You maintain this artificial barrier when it suits you. In the mid 90's CNN, and VOA were beaming life images all over world of the case of the Otokoto murder and the Owerri people's outrage against the gang of murderers. 1996 guys, not even in the age of the wireless systems. We in Nigeria did not own hand phones, only when family members residing abroad started calling Nigeria did we know what USA and the whole world had already seen and known. That was how we knew the world was watching. Can you imagine, an American presenter trying to pronounce OTOKOTO? I will finish this story at the end.

Welcome to the world my people. Welcome to a world that keeps accurate history of the times it has lived and the successes and failures thereof, but a world that will never seem to learn from its failings in history. Why do we have the power of thought, or memory, the power of recall and the ability to put life in perspective, which other lower life forms cannot do. Creation had gifted man the wisdom to husband the earth, to subdue the earth and to make a paradise for life on earth. Religion assures us, the other place where life exits is in the world where we can never go with this physical body; Heaven or Hell, Nirvana, Ala-mmuo, Paradise, whatever it is called in various religions, the thought is still the same. Biafra native religion refers to it as the land of our forefathers or the land of souls. To enter it, we must be found worthy of a meaningful life here on earth before we are admitted there after death. Science has tried, is trying still to find another planet in the myriads of stars across limitless space. Until such a life is physically found or until another planet is able to supply earth like characteristics, granting us another physical home, we have no other home than planet EARTH. This means that we have a duty to husband this earth for the benefit of mankind.

Human thought, wisdom and convictions are more diverse than the diversity of our clear racial divide of colors: black at one extreme and white at the other extreme. We cannot agree on everything is a fact, so the best thing to do is to accept that some differences cannot be breached by force; we must make do with what we have on our own and let the others be. The western world is tired of us, and have decided to abandon us in our moment of need. They must

as well leave our wealth and stop supporting, with weapons, those among us who do not help to develop our nations.
Today's question seeks to ask the world why history must be repeated, over and over again, if existing laws has a loophole, the responsibility of leadership is to prescribe a remedy or in the alternative enact a law to fill this loophole.

Who determines the facts of a situation that should not have arisen?

Whose responsibility is it to raise a finger and call for help when injustice is perpetrated by common will of the mighty, over the weak?

Who determines the weaker party and or which party needs protection in society?

What criteria is required to be established, so that a people laboring under the tutelage of a determined political group can be given protection, especially when both groups are not intrinsically one or assumed as being one by accident of political effectiveness?

What can an innocent group of people do when they are surrounded, a large hole dug and they are being beheaded one after another?

Who is responsible for collating and analyzing evidence sent-in online?

Even when we know that for one video or picture uploaded online, millions of such activities were not recorded or filmed. Perpetrators only take picture when they glory in their wickedness or feels justified by an errant law. History is being repeated here and the entire world looks the other way. Let us start our exploration from second world war. A nation decided to exterminate a class of people differentiated by race and their religious identity. The world saw it as a problem of that nation alone and until Japan attacked

America, the different nations could not be troubled apart from neighbors who were drawn in only when Germany threatened or attacked them specifically. Many of those European nations actually sent ethnic Jews to Germany for extermination.

In 1966, a varied unit of army officers launched a coup d'etat in Nigeria, the country selected an ethnic group for extermination. When Biafra tried to protect itself, Nigerian nation fought with the help of the then world super powers United Kingdom, Russia and others, to annihilate the Biafrans. I would not talk about how wars help 'weapon producing nations' to sell their weapons and make money on the back of oceans and rivers of blood, the super powers are the weapon producing nations then and now.

Khmer rouge was an ideology backed by neighboring countries to Cambodia. Pol Pot during his 1975 -1979 leadership exterminated more than 2 million of Cambodian citizens, selecting the learned, professionals and educated citizens first. Even the world coined a word 'KILLING FIELDS' I assume the feel of those two worlds merited better attention than the suffering and dying class of people in Cambodia.

The Tutsi and Huttu uprising which led to the summary execution of a less populated tribe by its own neighbors in Rwanda. Again it felt fine for the world to let the killings play out well over two months, so that there will be a load of pictures and evidence to document in our blood thirsty history, than to launch pre-emptive actions to save the two million people killed by a compatriot ethnic group.

In Congo, it is not clear to tell whether power thirst or resource control for the benefit of the super powers had led to a protracted war over several decades and till date Congo has never fully recovered still. Conflict still rage there much like the seasons. Summer-winter-autumn-spring, like that: Pogrom-warlords conference-unsteady peace-refugee-crisis; like that in a vicious circle it repeats in a three to four year cycle.

We had Kosovo, we had Bosnia and Hezegovania too. They are all ethnic groups bound by domiciliary constraints. Serbs, Slavs, Albanians, Bosnians, Croats and others, yet they were as brutal as any ethnic cleansing anyother place on earth. At the town of Srebrenica , more than 7,000 Bosniaks (Bosnian Muslim) boys and men, were massacred by Bosnian Serb forces while the United nations peace keepers looked on (out-numbered). Do your own homework, what monument would you raise to appease the blood-thirsty earth so that these killings would stop. None! but to sit up and draw up a new set of laws when the right to life, right to fair trial and right to freedom of worship in the United nation declaration of human rights can no longer guarantee life as we are witnessing.

Those stories peddled by the west about how many leaders of third countirs are supposed to be evil, cannibals and corrupt are no longer valid because now we know that many of these media houses are complete liars. They make up stories and demonize men who refuse to be puppets or submit to western propaganda. They collude with Europeans and America to lay waste to Africa so they would get access to African wealth and resources. Western nations are fantastically corrupt.

Gowon took almost all of Nigerian central bank to United Kingdom. Umaru Dikko transferred all monies meant for food importation to UK. Abacha's loot are still being recovered from all over Europe, decades after he looted Nigeria and stacked all in Europe. Who can tell why they demonized Idi Amin of Uganda? I hope you are watching Museveni today, soon a Mobutu Sese Sekou may arise and the cycle of violence will escalate. What did Zimbabwes's president do but nationalize his nations resources for the entire citizens of his country. Why would Europe and United Nations cry over this? Who own the land? What a farse "Landless blacks?" There are no landless blacks, because land is what and who we are. We are bonded to our lands and our culture and our home.

Liberia was a power tussle, the world left it to play for a few years then West African regional group went in. A generation of people were destroyed, the war spilled over to Sierra-leone. The world, nicely and in their supposed gentlemanly way of assumed political correctness waited for Charles Taylor at the Hague Court. What of the destroyed nations and its millions of citizens? I hope it is not now providing another arena for resource exploitation on the glorified rebuilding plan.
Afghanistan was left for the Soviets to create a battle of wits and in the process they developed a generation of fighters who took religion as their fighting model. When you kill them they win, if they kill you they still win. We were all sitting and watching our televisions when Saddam and Ayatollah started bickering over nothing, then they fought for eight years, We still waited till Iraq annexed Kuwait before we went in and in the process unleashed terror for those spawn in the Afghan caves and mountains to have a second fighting arena.
Do you still remember how the Arab spring began, when a poor worker who has lost his job was so sad that he launched a one-man protest against austerity by setting himself on fire. But, do not tell me you didn't know the years of poverty, reckless suppression of freedom and enduring suffering of the peoples in most of the areas affected by the Arab spring. We know but it was on the other side of the fence. Same inattention gave us the Syrian war, which is raging even as I write now. Why haven't Syrian war been classified as the fourth world war. Iraq was Third world war of course. Only thing remaining to be used in Syria today is the atomic bomb. Libya on my mind. Let me pretend that I do not know the advancement in world weapons race as at today. Yemen is now a regional war and when we hear of missiles we think it is far away. Yes, they are far away but still they fall into people's homes and lives, they take away loved ones, hopes and aspirations and they shatter our peace no matter how far away we may be.

You are watching chains and series of pictures and videos of the carnage in Nigeria. Yes ethnic cleansings, killings that are basically genocides of one ethnic group against the other. Trust the world, they coin it as herder and farmer conflicts which had always been there but now have aggravated due to climate change. Why are we so stupid? Those people who make up false stories at the mainstream media are just like you and I, only they are more evil and paid to change the narratives. We should not listen to their rubbish trying to hoodwink us so they may control the rancor amongst us, as a way to continue installing puppets in our state houses. I want you to remind me again how long France have been buying Resources from French West African nations and how much France paid for those resources. Please remind us again why France has to be the bank of all its former colonies directly running the country with the barrel of the gun.

You need to know that the lowest cost of an AK47 is between 500 - 800US dollars; that is Nigerian naira 180,000 to 288,000 naira (2021 price). A country classified as the poverty capital of the world, a shit-hole country a zoo as our leader addresses it for obvious reasons. Now do you still believe that cattle herders can afford to buy these weapons? Some of these weapons in some of the videos on the internet have the paint of the Nigerian armed forces and police. If you do a few calculations based on the different videos posted since 2011, it is an average of 100 people killed per week. With a peak of 500 people murdered in some major attacks. The Myetti Allah group had declared sometime ago, they will kill 300 people in plateau state. The said statement was made after killing more than 100 people few days prior. The dead, missing, comatose president of Nigeria, now replaced by some aberration called Presidency, have been silent and very unresponsive to these attacks. At a point, he said he did not know his army chief did not follow his orders. Back at his home-town, on a day he was visiting Katsina state, about 600 school boys were gifted to terrorists and later returned by the supposed terrorists in exchange for trillions of dollars ransom. Yet he can launch a brutal army operation against Biafra while trying to provoke a reprisal in other to start Nigeria/Biafra War II. ***(Nwa nnunu na agba awa tinyo n'okporo uzo, nwere onye n'akuru ya egwu")***. The dancer we can see at the center of the road is listening to a drummer somewhere even if we cannot see them. United Kingdom is that drummer, the United Nation too is that drummer. We are summarily brutalized and executed for being Biafrans. Your (United Nations), deafening silence even when "End-SARS" protesters demanding better governance were massacred is very telling. It is now the middle belt 'Christian majority' states of Plateau, Benue, Taraba and others. For the killings in Zaria and Kaduna, I also believe the United Nations calls that an internal matter or a police action by a responsible government.

The world is now tired of immigrants flooding into Europe so the best option is to hold leaders of these nations accountable to the World and not to its people. The behavior of a bad leaders leads to desperate migration of their people into your countries, so hold these leaders accountable to ensure they are responsible to their people. Is this asking too much? Is this an impossible feat? Why would a few persons reserve the right to kill, maim, rape, impoverish and degrade their own people while the world watch. I do not believe that such a possible law is impossible to describe, impose and implement; unless of course some WEAPON PRODUCING NATIONS AND ECONOMIC EXPLOITER NATIONS KNOW THEY WOULD LOSE FREE LOOTING RIGHTS they are carrying out in these nations. We should not export our citizens to Europe by a war that should not exist in the first place. There is a clear method of immigration, but my worry is not immigration, it is the lives wasted on the sands of Nigeria by Nigerian government through police and army in connivance with Boko Haram, ISWAP, Bandits and Fulani herders all with the complicit silence of the international community. We must point fingers when issues grow horns.

And for that early story of Ted Turner and the CNN I began with, in this age when a primary school child would dribble his parents with the networks. When my son in secondary school can write programs for a computer game, when we live-stream a walk in the garden, teenagers lives-stream orgies and their endless challenges. Well, when I can make video calls across any stretch of distance on planet earth, you mean you want me to believe and assume that Isha Sesay who pulled Nigerian generals apart exposing lies and deception during the Chibok girls saga had retired? Richard Quest does not travel again? Amanpour and all the award winning investigative journalists had suddenly changed suits? Have the dark continents fear of malaria taken new hold? So now, at once, media equipments have contrived to break down making Biafran sufferings not news worthy. All of a sudden, the people who gave the world Phillip Emeagwali do not deserve to live in their own homes and on their lands? The parents, brothers and sisters and relations of Kanu Nwankwo, J.J. Okocha, Peter Konyekwachie, Mikel Obi, and many others. The Biafrans on your streets, and factories, workers in every fields of professional life serving in your nations are affected. Lest I forget, they have brought to you more professionals per ratio of immigrant ethnic group. The silent masters of their work, well then, what are you waiting for. We have not crossed any thresholds, we did not carry guns until our lives were threatened, we are not terrorists, we just need to live free in peace and we must have it regardless of what you think. Chukwu Okike Abiama, the origin of all things, knows all things. Biafra deserves its own homeland and the answer is not Nigeria. When they wake up, tell those news satellite networks that even from the afterlife, truth will forever win.

What is holding Nigeria together?

Sometimes our leaders are not only short sighted but down right blind. There is nothing you can say to convince them, so my present mental disposition is to fight my cause to the best of my abilities and let history tell it all. MNK is entirely correct right now and given the Nigeria as it is structured he would have been correct in 1971 as well as will be in 2069 in the future. Archbishop Obinna, when he was a young priest moderated a leadership retreat for NFCS at Alvan Ikoku Owerri Campus, I attended as a representative of my college then. The highlight of the three days retreat was the struggles by the Catholics in Kaura Namoda polytechnic 1988/1989. At the time of the conference, the problem was still on going. Whether a church would be built, how high would the roof and a cross on top of it be. This had led to killings and closures of the school, resulted in religious crisis in the town and across the northern states. Till this day (2024), no politician has been able to conclusively address religious intolerance at Kaura Namoda. I have not mentioned resource control, good governance, infrastructural development, education and the issue of correct states. I have not mentioned health care industry and the metal ceiling placed on every Igbo man. Please Archbishop Arinze, have you solved the Ahiara issue politically or with religious spirit, have you researched the root causes of the Ahiara issue that it may not spill over as a church tradition. I know you would, I have the utmost respect for you intellectually. Spiritually you are my father too, but in the matter of Biafran self-determination, please I beg to disagree WE ARE CORRECT THIS TIME my Lord. A word of wisdom is important here: ***"odughu ife imere ka obi di onye iro mma"*** (there is nothing you will do to appease someone who hates you). Even if you die, the enemy will still be angry that you are not alive so he can see and enjoy your sufferings. IPOB need your support Archbishop, look critically on the matter at hand from every angle, there are no short fixes, who will rise up for the people if not us, who?

The same way the world abandoned the Tamils of Sri Lanka is the same way they are treating the Ambazonia and Biafra. It has nothing to do with religion and race. The world only responds to "interests," if there is sufficient interest then sorry if you happen to fall into the opposite site to the INTERESTS. Russia may actually be right in its intervention in Syria. Not like King Leopold did to Congo. UN is presently engaged in China's Coronavirus. Same thing happening in Yemen. This gives me a lot of reasons to doubt the whole UN hullabaloo and rhetorics about Palestine. So the Christians and Biafrans in Nigeria are less human? No not at all. They have shared the important resources of these nations. So sorry our people just happen to be on the other side of the divide, what will happen if we arm ourselves, because now we will.

Buhari is 'the dog and the baboon that would be soaked in blood!' He is correct because ***ochu nwa okuku nwe ada!*** Once we are able to say it as it is, our work is done. But we must keep talking so that those who have ears may hear, as for the understanding thereof; special divine intervention is not necessary all that is needed: arms and willingness to use it. They are teaching the next generation of war-mongers how it is done. This is only on earth this time....

Even Pope Francis know it and they are all hiding their heads in the sand, *unless we fight back, unless we fight back, and unless we fight back on time and do so with a more determined sense of purpose with greater ferocity than them, we shall not survive their onslaught*. One murdered today, two the next day, twelve the third day and so on. Do we actually think the numbers will stop or increase? Official government tally is around 20,000 murdered with tens of millions displaced. Are we learning to count? Do we not realize that this is GENOCIDE?

When will this counting exercise be tallied? What total are we looking for? At what number do we determine it? Yes may I ask, are you also counting material and psychological losses too? Some middle belt peoples will never be the same again while we are doing this addition exercise. Even TY Danjuma have been traumatised to the highest level (I do not mind him because he had a hand in the 1966 to 70 genocide against Igbo's as the world turned a blind eye, much as it is doing today again).

The crux of the matter today is to halt a genocide that is happening right now. Being politically correct would lead to another world war. Call a spade a spade and nothing else. Nigerian government is responsible for what is happening not Boko Haram, not bandits, not herdsmen. Nigerian government is guilty of carrying out a covert operation to exterminate a section of it's own people. If this is not true what else is. I will say it as our ancient Igbo proverb had: Only a tree would stand there and do nothing after hearing it would be cut down. Biafra will not stand and wait for death, since we live, we breath, we bleed so we will fight back.

Things happen at their appointed times. We have a lifetime to live and we must not plan for today alone. We should plan for that lifetime, even as we are not aware when it starts or when it may end. But then, as much of it as we are aware of, we must plan to the extent providence allows us to, that is our lifetime. Best laid out plans will fail, plans made without a thought to our mortality will fail too. Only real plan that would serve its purpose within the ambit of our live-able lifetime, is a plan made to survive to the point of our exit, but also affords our next of kin a leeway into their own next step. Therefore, as we listen to the clamouring in Syria and its response with gunfire, missiles and bombardment, we see a group of nations flexing their muscles there also, from America to Russia and many in between. To the tears, the response with gunfire, missiles and bombardment of Congo and Ambazonia. Iraq,

Libya and Somalia have not yet stabilised from the trauma of 1990's and early 2000's assaults. Now we can be sure that nations and not only people go through a long time of PTSD following a radical period of upheaval; yet many regions are not learning from the trauma of others. In fact, the thirst for conflict seems to be ingrained in our human DNA. Such that MAN courts strife, seeks it out, listens in the silence of peace for the drums of war; which are strummed repeatedly by people for whom the daily laughter of children and the natural rhythms of native life is ANATHEMA. People who do nothing but crave for the resources of their neighbors, those that derive pleasure from the pains and pangs of destruction, that see progress only when it walks on home streets. THEY WILL NEVER HAVE IT. Look carefully my friend, you can see the future theatres of conflict in Nigeria, the war mongers are keeping it on hold so that they may take time to utterly destroy the present houses of conflict. Then they would carry their war machines down to Nigeria. But why do we listen to the dogs of war, why do we dance to the call of the hounds when they roar in the dead of nights? We should wage peace when war is proclaimed to us from the blood stained pulpits of the weapon factories. We should reach out with conditions and find acceptable settlement before even the arrival of the evil dancers. How should we do this?

Hong Kong has been thrown into chaos every weekend for seven long weeks today and counting. If China comes up today and deliver a legendary address tomorrow morning; redefining the status of Hong Kong and Taiwan in such a way that these nations are free to pursue their singular aspirations as sovereign states, the natural race and creed and language and history of these nations will still forever remain as it has always being CHINESE. But China would have achieved the greatest peace ever in human history without a round table, without a single shot and without any deaths, and they would have the best of friendly relations with these nations forever. If Nigeria and Cameroon announce today the passage of laws which puts into play, a period for referendum and subsequent creation of Biafra, Oduduwa and Arewa nations amongst others for Nigeria and Ambazonia for Cameroon. Will our collective DNA automatically denature itself? Catalonia on one hand and in many other places too, like the Kurds etc. Who told you, your greatness and success and stability as a nation and a people, is dependent on being bound to a people and an area that would not assimilate with you? Nature has immiscible substances, so also does it have people who cannot or would not assimilate with you. Why do you think your existence is threatened by the freedom and possible success or failure of another? I dare to say Malaysia unitarily freed Singapore in the 1960's barely 5 years into single union nationhood. Today both countries have survived and do consider each other brothers more than you can imagine. Millions of Singaporeans and Malaysians cross the causeway each day. I know if any of this two nations is radically threatened from outside; each would stand shoulder to shoulder to support the other. They did not fire, have not fired a single bullet to achieve what they have today, so why does the Hausa/Fulani assume that without the oil from the bight of Biafra they would cease to exist. Why wouldn't the Kurds, the Ambazonians, the Houthis, the Syrians, Hong Kong walk free as they please. Because we humans, have evil bottled up in us, to seek to destabilize our near neighbor, defined by racial or ethnic differences. Because we seek to enslave others even if it means holding ourselves hostage. History however will never stop to teach us its truth because the down trodden never accept defeat, as far as there is a will, a way would show itself.

In the meantime let the evil drummers keep up their destructive work, someday a Cyrus would rise up as King and HE would declare, without a referendum and the war machine, "Let the peoples return to their natural homelands and be unto themselves a nation in peace." The stronger power should not call the weaker to a conference, in the heart of every man is embodied a spiritual conscience to discern every fact, every situation, every circumstance of lived experience amongst his people. Let go of dishonest rhetoric, irresponsible hullabaloo, useless conditions and standards. Only the truth shall set you free. No amount of force can buy you loyalty, a slave today maybe yet resistance will go on, until freedom is achieved. Biafra shall be free!

Part of the reason why Nigeria is not making a success like her mates is primarily because we seem to have cultivated a culture of celebrating wealth. That is not bad in itself, after all, there are certain cultures that worship money yet they are not in the sorry state we find ourselves in. The issue stems from irresponsibility in our approach to duty. We lack a national sense of duty....

I just lost my will to continue this article. Someone said that what Fela's songs protested in the 1970's are still issues on board today. Another pulled a Gani Fawehimi article from the 1980's that seems to have been written yesterday. To make matters worse, the names of a few current leaders of the people today were in those articles of decades ago. The *Newswatch* magazines and old daily newspapers should be reprinted from the date: 1987, they are all current affairs of today 2019 to 2023. Therefore, I have lost my zeal to speak or even write or contend the lack of progress of your nation Nigeria.

The only thing that we seem to have kept abreast of other nations or even surpassed many others are the spate of killings by, murderous fulani herdsmen, kidnapping by gangs of abandoned youths/(manpower that should have been trained to be meaningfully engaged in the job of nation building). We have Wanton desecration of the principles of religion through irresponsible mastery of oratory and deceit. The level of destructive tendencies in the country today exceeds some war zones elsewhere in the world. Why do we not have functional stadiums to enable sports development and engagement of our youth in that aspect of human endeavor, but we have hundreds of churches which buildings seats hundreds of thousands of worshippers? Why are there no companies and manufacturing concerns, healthy SME's and local enabling strategies, government industrial reserve areas to kick start local investments, encourage international investors too, but we have an ever increasing pool of schools, universities, polytechnics, colleges of education that are seasonally turning out thousands of graduates yearly, are we asking why?

Well as I started above, lost interest. I do not wish to be another voice that will rise, live and die at old age with the system not even acknowledging the words of the masters. I prefer to revisit those masters of whom I spoke about and recycle their words and speeches, which are still vividly current today as when they were uttered 30 to 40 years ago... stay put and read them..., Biafra shall be free.

To Understand is another matter

We never win when we believe we have. A reason I love going through the first five books of the old-testament. Everything we are experiencing in the world today is bottled up in there. There is nothing added and nothing removed. The problem is that we read but we do not understand. We do not understand because we have already assumed the knowledge we want, nothing else goes into our minds. We would not let it. No why would I listen to that, why would I even contemplate that there may be any good out of listening. These days when 'Whatever' has lost its sting, what we do now is to pretend that it never happened, we did not hear about it, or it does not matter at all. Whatever it may be or mean, really matters. The wise one said, many had hosted angels unawares and went on to reap endless good fortunes they could not account for otherwise. Well then, the Igbos say: "**onye ajuru aju anaghi aju onwe ya**" (an outcast cannot cast himself out).

I have picked on this verse before: 'an unexamined life is not worth living'. Many of us go through the motions of living without trying to make of themselves someone meaningful to benefit either themselves or human kind. We cannot afford to be like that, there must be a definition of yourself, by you and for you. You must determine who you are, before you can say 'this is me.' We are called by the names we give out to people. We can say I am Iwunna but for all purposes and intent behave like Chidi, people will call me Chidi because they are seeing and dealing with Chidi.

There are no two ways to it, there is also no better ways to put it and there is nothing to hide about it if we are now an endangered community. We practice a faith because of which everywhere we are seen, we are cut down unceremoniously. Why? Well, because you think our faith commits us to love and forbear arms and to live in brotherly love?

I beg to differ my people. They who advance this type of dogma, have really not looked into the bible properly.

It says 'I came to bring division, nation against nation, father against son, mother against daughter.'

In another place it say 'but now, he who has no sword, sell his cloak and buy a sword'.

Again it tells of when the bridegroom is with you and when the bridegroom is taken away from you?

Finally, let me quote for you 'I said it before, now I am sending you out as sheep among wolves, you must be gentle as a dove but wise as a serpent.'

I am not your bible teacher, be that as it may, Igbo say: ***"Ukpana okpoko gburu nti chiri ya."*** Look around, take examples from nations that have some semblance of justice and peace in them, learn from them. No one really appreciates the difference till they step out of their homes then look in from outside.

The cage is not on the outside it is in your mind. Yes! Think first. Though the shoes binding our legs pinch and hurt us, if we do not try to walk without them, we would not know if we could make do without them.

Biafra shall be free....

When I wrote here that our work is to write and write and educate our people, I knew that was absolutely empowering. Did you see the resistance to election rigging? It is not yet over. Let us keep showing our people what we all need to know in other to better our lots keep writing people forget the mainstream media being paid to hide truth and deceive people with lies. Write and write and write. Share truth when you see it especially video evidences. Be ready with your phones to record and send online. Only our efforts can change our destinies. Yes, the success may seem little now but do not worry, time will vindicate the truth. If we now know the difference from politics and demands of governance. We cannot allow our collective destinies to become politics. We need good governance we do not need politics... Biafra shall be free!

You know some people are justifying their mistakes by claiming lack of wisdom at the time. Well a mistake is a mistake, the best thing we can do is to accept responsibility and determine not to fall for it again. Let me tell you; the situation in 1819; is just as different from 2019 because of the difference in persons facing issues on those specific dates. If one had decided to make a false decision granting the knowledge available at the time in 1819; if you bring him to 2019 and give him the knowledge available in 2019 he would still make a bad decision. It is as simple as that. If you had voted for Buhari in 2015 well of cos 98% of Igbo did not vote him (97% and 5% saga) there is a chance you can redeem yourself this election by rejecting his brother Atiku, and his anointed successor Tinubu. There is no other time for recalling bad leadership. If you call it a mistake this second time around, (well that is why we have individual autonomy please be clear on this), it is your choice not mistake. Let us not try at all. How is it that we have to try, try, try, what trying is that? With our time and collective destinies. How many persons have tried to cut their legs with a hoe; yes we know the knife cuts, but try with a hoe or try with a chisel, no, no attempt to cut your leg with a log. You know its blunt but yes, let us try it. Have you tried running into a tree? Yes if the car drives and hits a tree it will crash. What if I just run into a tree, or again, let us roll into the ocean not dive. They are two different things. Not dive, let us try rolling and see if the ocean will still drown us. So why would you try giving the entire Nigeria into the hands of someone whose brother is determined to kill everyone. Tell me the difference between half a dozen and six. Our mumu still remain... only in Nigeria .... well we are not even going to vote that day at all.

Following a certain outburst after the Buhari/Osibanjo expose I commented thus:

So when he could not find his certificate and you preferred him to a doctorate degree holder, what were you thinking. Buhari should win a second time and really deal with us in such a way that we will start valuing education. They put a soldier who could not tell if he finished secondary school as opposed to a doctorate degree holder, a university lecturer, before you to choose who will lead you and you chose the former. Tell me on what basis did you, the complainant, vote for Buhari. On what basis, ethnicity or religion, his humanity or compassion on what basis was Buhari elected? Shut up and enjoy the ride! I screamed till my voice was no more still he won yes it is democracy let him show you what you voted for.

Again, I commented:

Now you can see why education is important. There is nothing more important than giving or getting the best education possible whether it is through formal or informal systems. We can see what we have done to ourselves.

Someone defended the status quo thus:

Dear Augustine, the issue of certificate or who superintends between Buhari and Osinbanjo should not arise here. Firstly, the Vice President, Osinbanjo from the word 'go' knew he was to be the running mate to our indefatigable president. He was aware educationally, he is privileged to be a Ph.D. (Law) holder, which invariably meant that 'all things being equal' he is most qualified to lead in that direction and yet, he swallowed the whole thing line, hook, and sinker. He accepted to be under Buhari. That was a plus for him. At least, even if he does not ascend to the highest throne of the land after 8 years, he would be referred to as 'Former Vice President' of Nigeria. After all, some people do not mind being a president or vice president of a country even for 24 hours. Secondly, bro the slot for the position of the president by the party was predicated on the fact that such person must come from the North. Osinbajo is from the South West and the issue of who has better qualification should not arise. The presidential candidate was, or is the best the North could then provide for the country and everybody embraced him hence his success on the polls. So, let us wish them well in their current or future endeavors. Another time has come for you to remake or unmake what you made before now. Good luck to you all!

My reply:

Why, there are systems and processes in life, even when we know that there are exception to every rule. We live in the same country, we buy from the same market, we have families and friends who are in the same country. We know there are graduates of English language who are not proficient in English. As a matter of fact, we may know sometimes natural wisdom can eclipse intelligence but then these and other related issues are incidental and not the norm. No matter how intelligent a young man of thirty can be there is a greater wisdom in a wizened old man of 70. That is predicated on the older man being sane, properly traditionally educated and lived a meaningful life through which he has acquired the wisdom accruing due to age. However, in terms of those systems and processes, in terms of administrative efficiency, in terms of the zeal to meet challenges and the strength to carry out pledges, inspire confidence and engage the development of the present. A youth at forty to forty five would far out-perform his grandfather. In reference to a youth of 45, I have in mind, a careful controlled and intelligent man driven by the passion to make a statement in the lives of his people. A man of compassion and wisdom who feels the plight of his generation. In whatever thing we do, we move in holding onto the truth of the situation. Believing that the exception can also be true is not correct. That is why it is known as an exception and not the basis for decision-making. We in Nigeria have this assertion: "does he feed me!" Implying that our personal ability to cater for ourselves is evidence that we do not need a lawyer, we do not need a doctor, we do not need an engineer, we do not need a teacher, and so on. What a catastrophic assumption. You can see where it is keeping us today. There is a reason the four walls of the school would instill greater wisdom not only intelligence on a person who had been there, than one who dropped out or never went in. Degrees and certificates are awarded based on "having successfully passed and allowed the institution to pass through" the arguments that the other engineer cannot repair a car is only true for lack of practical experience. Put him to work and see. For he learnt the principles with minimal practical experience. But the car works on principles only, intake- compression- power- exhaust-; when he finally get to work, the pieces would fall into place simple;

there is no comparison at all; because you would compare the best in the two arms of learning you cannot compare a "let my people go" graduate of mechanical engineering with an excellent road side Mechanic. Therefore, let us accept that we made a colossal wrong choice from the beginning. I tell you in truth "the conditions, the successes the failures, the development and future of a people lies in their hands only" if we keep covering our faces like the ostrich to bury our heads in the sands our problems will forever remain our problems. Until we decide enough is enough, that is when our irresponsibility would be determined. I am not interested in how many people are falsely empowered, calculate it, our time runs in a decade between leaders and tell me when that exception would be picked out. (I know 4 + 4 is 8). The truth is that simple period.

Look around you, a high percentage of Biafrans live in the diaspora, make a simple comparison and decide for yourself. If we attain soveregnity of our Nation, would Biafra achieve greatness or not? So what is preventing that?

We need more involvement over this matter because we have to educate our people. Major problem we have in Nigeria is that we are caught up with the present. Let's look at it this way; if you are 20 years old today, you have a promise of 50 years in the future. If you are thirty you have a promise of 40 years. If you are forty you have a promise of thirty years, if 50 years old today you have a promise of another 20 years. It is an unspoken promise, a promise that is dependent on our way of life and by Destiny. A lot of people would not obtain this promise by no fault of theirs at all, but for majority of humanity this is the case. How then do we prepare for these coming years? If we do nothing to adjust our positions, tomorrow would meet us and we would not be ready for it, simply because we did not shape both ourselves and the time to come. Yes by building strong institutions, we are shaping tomorrow. But our leaders would misappropriate our resources for wasteful ends and we do nothing, we are not shaping the future the correct way. We would not pick up relevant skills looking at the trend of events today, tomorrow would meet us without the skills to thrive in it. Systems are being upgraded all over the world, for a time when the internet and electronic highway becomes the market world, business methods, cashless society and healthcare delivery, education becomes intensely personalised but what do we do in Nigeria? Strikes, forced on the system by irresponsible government, the irresponsible government being cropped up by ethnic and religious bigotry. Youths who have been trained not to care for their future become foot soldiers of the few, who want the destruction to continue. If we do not prepare for tomorrow, definitely we would not be ready for what is coming at us. Let us wake up today. The trick is believing that we can do something if we earnestly want to. Change in all the leading countries of the world was not achieved by lying to themselves. They worked for it. Not by fighting the differences amongst them but by letting go so that there is unrestrained growth. We can all achieve our potentials only if we really want it strongly enough and do something definite about the country.... Break up Nigeria now, Biafra shall be free.

At a time in life, someone is expected to take certain steps, behave in certain ways and take full responsibility of his or her destiny. Nigeria WILL NEVER live up to that expectations. Yes, it is going down. When that happens and we who have no voices, knowing that we would not go down for nothing decides to take a stand and extricate ourselves from a suicide match. I want to ask: what right do you have to decide my own stand if you have heartily made your decision without recourse to my own opinions?

Let that be noted, this country have been producing lawyers before independence. I want to know how many lawyers have effectively explained to a section of his/her people or the public of Nigeria, the full extent of the SOCIAL CONTRACT theory, which establishes a nation, and which if abused, means that parties to this contract have lost their positions in the contractual bonds they both must bear.

In all the years of misgovernance by the millitary and their cohorts by which I mean the educated class who form the tink-tank for military dictators of the past, what preparations was made to instill good moral standards and civic responsibility to the national psyche?

Now there was a ready partnership between religious leaders and the government, yes, interreligious dialogues as a national fixture, to which allusions are made from time to time. I need to know, APART FROM THE VEHICLES AND BUILDINGS ERECTED AND BURSARIES TO THE DIFFERENT HEADS, what religious conflicts have ever been amicably settled without a loss of life and which religion in Nigeria knows a thing about tolerance?

The traditional leaders too have failed to checkmate the steady decline of truth, honor, love, trust, hope, faith, and perseverance in the pursuit for titles. Some kingdoms remain empty for several years while rivals are silenced by any means possible. Are you not part of the problem?

In times past when I lived in the tales of the fore-fathers, youths are mightily organised as the strength of the clan. They wait on the fringes of the ebo listening to the heated debate of the elders on the way forward. They bristled with raw energy and anger when the debates runs to common sense as elders decides to wait a case out for a rainy day. They were also known to have entered the evil forests in a daring move against the laws of the elders but in a bold consensus of the Mgbadike to challenge the ChukwuOkikeAbiama for a wrong... they always win. Today politics have destroyed every facet of social life in our society with the help of religion and royal institutions. You the youths, cannot read the signs of the times.

Stop listening to Soyinka or to Iwuanyanwu, to this or that organizations, they have no messages, stop listening to names and caps and feathers and staff of authorities that are meaningless... they have failed us, as much as United Nations too. I know how hard you work and how much you dream of a future. In the present structure of Nigeria, there is no road. It does not matter which religion you profess or which ethnic group you belong to, there is no future for Nigeria as it is presently structured and has been since before independence. There is nothing any one can do about it, not even with all the wisdom we can collectively muster can we change the status quo. Until we can live and let the other live, until you can aspire to be a tailor and tolerate some neighbor who wants to be a driver without a thought to it. Until you can build a hut and not bother a man who wishes to marry four wives, until you can pray to a tree and not bother a man who wants to pray to the sea, until the judge's position is merited and not zoned to Azikiwe's family. Until the lawyer takes a case and knows that the police did their best investigation, until the doctor is the best student and not richest student, and until the tout stops chasing cars on the streets for no just reason? There is no road. I am not in a hurry. He that sits astride me on the ground and swears he will not let me stand up, please brothers is he standing?

But for you the youths I have the greatest regrets, your silence, your acceptance that you have failed is yours and yours alone to bear. ONLY in Nigeria, Biafra shall be free!

Oluchi my friend, there will not be any usefulness to an Obi vice presidency to Ndigbo. The fulani that placed him there are not even happy to have him and his intellect on the table of governance at Abuja. He is there as a last resort to dampen the raging Biafran fires. With the disappearance of Nnamdi Kalu at the hands of Buhari still the agitation is raving mad, the aim now is to move towards a false offer. The people look at the table and some would say: "After all an Obi is there", but his presence will not even be acknowledged since he is Igbo. Maybe many of these fake leaders do not know it, we are all Biafrans to the entire Nigerian nation. An attempt to claim otherwise will make your position very dangerous out there in the open. Do you ever think that Rochas, Orji Uzo and other fake Igbo apologists will ever get Nigerian acceptance unless they descend so low as to betray their own people. That is what happened to the promise of Rochas and his group. He had to show that he is not an Igbo to his fulani friends by destroying Imo ruthlessly. Tell me what Obi can achieve. In the best he is just a VP. The single enduring problem we have is bringing NO historical perspective to matters of the future in the present. If Obi even goes in, he has automatically set Nigeria's development and progress back by another 30 years. Sit down and do a proper analysis how long it took from Ekwueme (VP) to Goodluck President; then remember how difficult it was for Goodluck. He had to repeatedly emphasize he is not Igbo, why? It is Goodluck's tenure that woke up vehemently the rage of the North to destroy Nigeria if they do not take the center from an "Igbo man". Obi himself is just playing a tune feeling accomplished to be chosen as VP. I have nothing against him, it is a personal accomplishment and he deserves to celebrate having reached that height, BUT for a people: NDIGBO; there could be no greater disaster than failure to seek self-determination when we are almost there. I give you an unrelated basic story everyone knows.

A man after years of hustle in Nigeria decided to travel abroad, he convinced his father to sell a land for this venture. His father asked him to get a wife before he travels to the USA. His cousin travelled immediately while he stayed home and married; then his father further asked that the wife should be pregnant before the man travelled. When the wife became pregnant, he started his visa process. With all the demands of the wife and stories he had heard that his cousin was still having establishment problems in the USA since he was not into fast deals, the man, he, began to doubt the wisdom of emigration as a means of self-determination. He reasoned to and did finally abandon the trip. Today after ten years only; he is still a tricycle driver but now holds a second job as guard to his cousin's country home in Nigeria. The same cousin that he should had travelled with. It is honest work at home, but we shelf personal and financial independence when we could have achieved it. That is the crossroads we are at today. Many have died and many more would follow. In the game of self-determination, there are no short cuts and there are no compromises. All or nothing. Obi's VP or Presidency, will set us back several generations. Nigeria had started this race with nations like Ghana, Malaysia, Indonesia, we even helped Southern Africa get independence but now we are not at par; maybe seeking a job to guard their country homes as in the story I told. Because we are saddled with a millstone on our neck (ethnicity and religious bigotry) while swimming the ocean of survival. You cannot drag someone that does not want to go anywhere with you. Cast off the yoke and fly Biafra! Only in Nigeria.

History must be learnt or suffered.

In the present times 31/8/18 when Malaysia is celebrating 61 years of independence. The national TV stations showed repeatedly the path to independence. All salient points where constructively argued and agreement reached. The initial major huddle was the status of Chinese and Indians, who arrived with colonialism. They were granted citizenship with affirmative action for the first nation Malays, added to so many other points, mind you there was civil strife, distrust, ethnic, religious and racial difficulties in Malaysia at the time prior to and soon after independence, but they finally agreed. For the success of one racial identity; the other race must also be accommodated. Today Malaysia is moving into the mainstream and still standing strong on their identity as one. Each individual ethnic group in Nigeria, I mean ethnicity, not racial divide, all natural born of Nigeria, believes that the other ethnic group is her problem. We allow religion to divide us; we think that we are not on the same levels as our brother but surprisingly some ethnicities will not want to go their separate ways. We must learn from other nations successes. Due to a consistent disagreement in parliament in the early days of nationhood, Singapore was expelled from Malaysia, and I tell you today both nations are on perfect friendly relations as brothers. They still have same demographic realities only at different levels. Malaysia (Singapore's main source of WATER) has honored water policies throughout till today with round table talks. Both nations cry together and smile together as family should. In your case, northern Nigeria wants southern oil and not the Southern people. They want the eastern industrial drive but not the Easterners. Western Nigeria wants to drive the easterners away after Lagos and Ogun states after these areas among others have been developed by the easterners. Eastern leadership are thieves who rely on the division at the top to develop myopic policies of looting and thuggery. The people are left to wallow in ignorance and lack of basic utilities. What is this we are doing to ourselves? We allow evil to flourish by letting western leaders and religious blocks keep directing the bad leaders we elect while they drain our resources. There is no other reason this is perpetrated on us by ourselves; other than the fact that wise men amongst us are not allowed to bring their thoughts to bear when it matters. Well, it is our responsibility to say NO! Mazi Nnamdi Kalu has shown the way and we must rise up and say Enough is enough. But mark it somewhere, even if it takes millions of years, if the peoples of Nigeria: Hausa Igbo Yoruba and the major and lesser minorities do not collectively strive to engineer a good separation, there would be continued blood bath and failure of nationhood. When other nations are moving towards easy management and control, we are still dragging land.

The morning was cool and quiet around 7am when I sat up in bed and crawled out leaving my wife snuggled there in bed. Our children were still sleeping in their rooms as I made my way downstairs. The palour was spotlessly clean, every fixture in its place, the tiles brightly reflect soft images of the objects around even in the near darkness of the room. I quietly stepped up to the double doors, switched a knob, then pulled the built in window half of the door open. More light streamed into the room at once and a cool draught of fresh breeze greeted me. I stood still and gazed out to my 12 feet by 3 feet shared space on the street edge acros from my house. The mata-kucing and mango fruit trees, stood also in place proclaiming our character to the community.

I had to think, the silence does not get to me again after eight months of total lockdown due to the ongoing covid 19 pandemic. The 'His and Hers' cars sat silently in their places, waiting for wife and I to put them to use, who knows when. There were no cars on the streets nor sounds of such in the distance. Even the plants stood perfectly still as if under command. Yes we are! I scanned the streets and beyond from left, where a recycling factory can be seen about 200 meters away, through across the different factories, stores and car display and sales pavilion to the main roundabout at my extreme left. No living soul was outside. The law has taken effect all over Malaysia. I saw on television yesterday, a few persons had raised white flag, as a signal for aids somewhere in Selangor and at few other areas. I waited for nothing, I expected nothing too because my wife and I having had difficult time in early marriage had worked hard and put in place a system through which we can remain self-sufficent for a period not less than ten years without needing physical or financial assistance from anyone. We worked for it. Pandemic was speaking to me now lost in thought, 'do I need to source for weapons for self-defence, in readiness for a trime when chaos will become the order of the day?'

Eight months of complete shut-down-order enforced by the Tentera Darat Malaysia? Welcome to the world my people. Welcome to a world that keeps accurate history of the times it has lived and the successes and failures thereof, but a world that will never seem to learn from its failings in history. Why do we have the power of thought, or memory, the power of recall and the ability to put life in perspective which other lower life forms cannot do. Creation had gifted man the wisdon to husband the earth, to subdue the earth and to make a paradise for life on earth. Religion assures us that the other place where life exits is in the world where we can never go with this physical body; Heaven or hell, Nirvana, Paradise or whatever it is called in various religions, the thought is still the same. Igbo native religion refers to it as the land of our fore-fathers. To enter it, we must be found worthy of a meaningful life here on earth before we are admitted there after death. Science has tried, is trying still to find another planet in the myriads of stars across the limitless space. Until such a life is physically found or until another planet is able to supply earth like characteristics granting us another home we have no other home than planet EARTH. That means that we have a duty to husband this earth for the benefit of mankind.

Human thought and wisdom, and conviction is more diverse than the diversity of our clear racial divide of colors: black on one extreme and white to the other extreme. I was so surprised the day I first saw a Chinese Albino. The only thing I thought of that day was that all humans were the same, no matter what science have to say about it. This conviction was not an easy one given that I, as a good scholar of genetics, had earlier believed cultural mix millions of years ago was to blame for the occasional similarity in thoughts and behaviors across racial and ethnic diversity. This is not true, we are humans and we are all the same.

Today's question seeks to ask the world why history must be repeated, over, and over again. If existing laws has an obvious loophole, would the responsibility of the leaders not be to prescribe a remedy or in the alternative enact a law to fill this loophole?

Who determines the fact of a situation that should not have arisen?

Whose responsibility is it to raise a finger and call for help when injustice is perpetrated by common will of the mighty over the weak?

Who determines the weaker party, and which party needs protection in society?

What criteria or what laws can save a group of people laboring under the tutelage of a determined political group, when both groups are intrinsically one or assumed as being one by accident of political effectiveness?

What can an innocent group of people do when they are helmed-in, a large hole has been dug and they are being beheaded one after another?

Who is responsible for collating and analyzing evidence sent-in online for legal purposes?

Even when we know that for one video or picture uploaded online, millions of such activities were not recorded of filmed. Perpetrators only take picture when they glory in their wickedness, or feels justified by an errant law.

History is being repeated here, and the entire world looks the other way. Let us start from the Second World War. A nation decided to exterminate a class of people differentiated by race and religious identity. The world saw this as a problem of that nation. And up until Japan attacked America without reasonable cause, the different nations could not be troubled, except neighbors who were drawn in only because Germany threatened them specifically.

In 1966, a group of army officers launched a coup d'etat in Nigeria, the country selected an ethnic unit for extermination, when the group tried to protect itself, the Nigerian nation fought with the help of then world super powers (Britain and their allies) to annihilate the Biafrans. I would not talk about how wars help 'weapon producing nations' to sell their weapons and make money on the back of oceans and rivers of blood, the super powers are the weapon producing nations then and now.

The Khmer rouge was an ideology backed by neighboring countries to Cambodia. Pol Pot during his 1975 -1979 leadership exterminated more than 2 million of Cambodian citizens, selecting the learned professionals and educated citizens first. Even the world coined a word 'KILLING FIELDS' I assume the feel of those two worlds merited better attention than the suffering and dying class of people in Cambodia.

In the Congos, it is not clear to tell whether power thirst or resource control for the benefit of the super powers led to a protracted war over several decades and till date Congo has never fully recovered still.

Liberia was a power tussle but the world left it to play for a few years, then regional group went in and out. A generation of people were destroyed, the war spilled over to Sierra leone, what good has Charles Taylor's arraignment at the Hague war crimes Court done to the millions dead or traumatized by that war. Who had identified or charged the nations that armed and urged on Charles Taylor: France, United Kingdom, United State? What of the destroyed nation? I hope it is not now providing another arena for resource exploitation on the glorified rebuilding plan.
Do you still remember how the Arab spring began, when a poor worker who has lost his job was so sad that he launched a one man protest against austerity by setting himself on fire. But don't tell me you didn't know the years of poverty, reckless suppression of

freedom and enduring suffering of the peoples in most of the areas affected by the Arab spring. We know but, it is on the other side of the fence. Remember who is in the habit of urging or creating the circumstances for Austerity measures, the World bank and their cronies. Inattention gave us the Syrian war, which is raging even as I write now. Why haven't Syrian war been classified as the fourth world war. Iraq was Third. Only thing remaining to be used in Syria today is the atom bomb. Let me pretend I do not know advancement in world weapons race as at today. Yemen is now a regional war and when we hear of missiles, we think it is far away. Yes! they are far away, but still they fall into people's homes and lives, they take away loved ones, hopes and aspirations, and they shatter our peace no matter how far away we may be. You are watching chains and series of pictures and videos of the carnage in Nigeria. Yes ethnic cleansing, now being excused as killings in the name of herder and farmer conflicts. When has climate change become war? What do you understand as farmer and herder conflict? These killings have been going on for more than 5 decades, so where is the farmer and herder conflict story coming from? Exactly from the terrorist mouthpiece of BBC, CNN, and other media houses pushing a wrong narrative to sideline the real issue of terrorism sponsored by United Kingdom, France and the USA with tacit support from the United nations simply to continue to milk African Natural resources. Just listen to Blinken, to Macron and to Antonio Gutteres for a while and reason into the unsaid or tacitly stated policies when they turn to Africa. Farmer and Herder conflict my foot.

An AK47 costs between 500 – 800 US dollars; that is Nigerian naira 180,000 to 288,000 Naira as at 2022. Do you still believe that cattle herders can afford to buy these weapons? Some of these weapons in the videos on the internet have the paint of the Nigerian armed forces and police. If you do a few calculations based on the different videos posted since 2011, it will give an average of 100 people killed per week, with a peak of 500 people massacred in some major attacks. The miyetti Allah group have declared that they will kill 300 people in plateau after killing more than 100 persons two days ago. The president of Nigeria have been silent and very unresponsive to these attacks. At a point, he said he did not know his army chief did not follow orders. Buhari launched a brutal army operation against Igbos: Operation Python dance, trying to provoke a reprisal in other to start Biafra War II. True to its form United Kingdom has effectively kept quiet on the whereabouts of its citizen, Nnamdi Kalu, who was thought to have been killed in that attack. All the others summarily brutalized and executed for being Igbos are of course no concern to the world, for so I would assume from your deafening silence even when they were unarmed protesters demanding better governance. It is now the middle belt 'christian majority' states of Plateau, Benue, Taraba and others, for the killings in Zaria and Kaduna, I also believe the United Nations calls that an internal matter or a police action by a responsible government.

The world is now tired of immigrants flooding into Europe so the best option is to hold leaders of these nations accountable to the World and not to its people. The behaviour of a bad leader, leads to a desperate move of its people into your own country, so hold that leader and ensure he is responsible to his people. Syria should not export its citizens to Europe by a war that should not exist in the first place. There is a clear method of immigration, but my worry is not immigration, it is the lives wasted on the sands of Nigeria by Fulani herders and a complicit National Government. I assume the western world tested the Ebola vaccine it developed in West Africa in 2014. I cannot prove it but there was a vaccine for “try-out” when the outbreak occurred such a lucky coincidence. Maybe you have reviewed Maltteus theorem and determined that world population needs a manual reordering, or new weapons of war need new KILLING fields for testing.

IF NOT WHAT ARE YOU DOING? You have ambassadors in Nigeria and they report back to you. So Buhari has convinced YOU that we are lazy, that we are thieves and criminals and so the world need to get rid of us! Remember there was a genocide where one party convinced its people that their neighbors are cockroaches, the rest is History. We need the law now... only in Nigeria

I heard the door knob turn, I remained fixed on my empty gaze while listening to my thoughts. I know my son an his mannerisms, he walked up and stood beside me looking out the door window with me.

“Anything Daddie?” he asked.

“No, nothing” I replied “was just lost in thought, what this pandemic may mean for life around us.”

“Would it had been better if we were back in Biafraland, you know our compound have everything, lands for gardening, fruit trees poultry and playgrounds?”

“No, it is best here, my thought is your admission to university, this ‘online thing’ cannot work for all courses, your course must be physical, practical is a must...” I purposely left it hanging giving him the chance to voice his own thoughts about the circumstances, so I can read his psychological preparedness for a long wait.

“Daddie the first year is all theory” he said.

“Mmmmmmmm, but they cannot go on with the theory without accommodating the other levels, everyone is affected.”

“True, I am not worried, something will come up I believe” he said much to my happiness.

“Yes they will find a way, call your siblings, the day is awake let us begin it well...”

I was now walking up the stairs to the master room, it is time to kiss my darling good morning.

The death match: THE STATE OF AFFAIRS OF A NATION REFLECTS THE WILL OF ITS PEOPLE.

This article targets political thugs, political servants, the police and officers of the election commissions. The civil servants who believe that they are reaping anything if the status quo remains the same. The directors in the state or federal ministries hoping to end up as permanent secretaries or commissioners as the case may be. The Eze's, Igwe's, Emir's and Oba's. Yes, there are many expectations we cherish and we hold on to these dreams even when every indication shows the contrary to be true. Maybe we think that other options lead to a more demanding pathway to success. That is lie. No success is achieved without genuine labor for it. Today Buhari has come out to call us every type of evil name on this earth, he has called us thieves (making him the President of thieves); he has called us lazy and stupid and idle and irresponsible (making him the President of lazy, stupid, idle and president of an irresponsible nation) but that is not the topic of today. I am trying to educate us, on that same verse which i keep repeating in many of my writings "the state of affairs of a people, a community, or a nation is exactly as the people want it to be." You may disagree, but look at the facts: the ruling class that sit on our millions refusing to use same resources to build infrastructures are from amongst us. They work with support staff of hundreds of assistants, bodyguards, police and their immediate trusted family members in other to maintain their positions. They have thugs who do their dirty work when ordinary intimidation from the police against their opponents fail to work. These thugs were groomed and empowered by them, in most cases are members of national security organizations. Yes! if you ask me to prove these assertions then you are one of them. What I am getting at is the fact that all the above mentioned, are members of that same community or nation which in this case is Nigeria. Our collective failure to challenge this anomaly in our country is direct acceptance of the status quo as law. We know that legal principles arises in several ways including; tradition, repetition, parliament and the judiciary. So we have by subtle acceptance to the repetition of bad governance actually accepted this to be the truth of our existence. To have evil men: thieves; murderers; liars; looters of public funds and unashamed criminals sit as our leaders. If you listen to a group of Nigerians argue about bad leadership you definitely will hear one respond "can you do a better job? ... we are all the same ... anyone you put in there will still steal and steal and steal ..." what an absurdity! There could not be any falsehood greater than this. The truth is that we have so become used to evil men's lies and deception that we tend to believe anything. Yes! every one of us know that 'no-nonsense teacher' living in our community; that strict disciplinarian who has turned his family into a success story even though he was just an ordinary shoe maker; we may know a nurse or doctor or lawyer who will never accept one kobo to change his or her principles. Yes, we may know a man who no one wants him to become the village Chief, because he will not wage an unnecessary war against the next village or bring out resources geared for community development for his friends to share, or give out contract without following due process. So then how can you say that we cannot from amongst ourselves get a leader who will be another Okpara, another Akanu Ibiam, another Iheonukara Mbakwe, another name it.

When Buhari was campaigning we knew his previous records, we had his full assertions that he will stop at nothing to carry out a vengeance against eastern Nigeria. We know his "making Nigeria ungovernable speech", we knew him like the back of our hands. So we wanted him, so we got him, now why should we complain. Eastern Nigeria rejected him in toto at the Aso rock Abuja; but then we went along and elected men at our various state houses; who does not have the political strength to withstand Abuja's on-slaught. Men who love wealth over their people, men who will further put us in misery... we have done so at every election since 1983 and at each succeeding year we become better at making bad choices. So all those in the election machinery who play very active roles, falsifying data after elections, of going to intimidate and or kill men who have done you no wrong, of chanting in the streets to support your own nemesis; have you thought about how you and your progeny will never have basic utilities of light and electricity forever? How your kids will never have the jobs they deserve? How the schools and hospitals will forever be empty, scary art works in our communities? Have you thought of how you will always be scared for your own personal safety? Have you thought of how life will always be a labor of tears for Nigeria and not beautiful scenes as we see in other countries?

They shout 'ethnicity' you rise up incensed and mad with your swords, you patrol the streets looking for the next Nigerian brother man to kill and pillage his hard-earned wealth. They scream 'religion!!!' and a generation of people arm themselves to the teeth and invade your neighbor slaughtering innocent children and women for no reason. But, you forget that your enemy is not on the streets. You put your own enemy in Aso rock and now you are on the streets, a ready missile that will burn itself out soon. Election is an ongoing process and until you get your act right, Nigeria! you will never have peace. It is not tribe, it is not religion, it is you who have decided that your state and country will never be good. People in Nigeria are once again campaigning for Buhari? They are Nigerians. People aided our expired state governors into the senate, not ghosts, people agreed in exchange for money and positions to influence the will of the people in the courts, in the offices. In our homes too, those decisions are being made. Let me tell you the results of your little gains today: your nation will never grow, your people will always be seen as evil and un-progressives, standard of living will forever be low. Life will be tough and a struggle for your own people and the future will be bleak. That is why Biafra must be free. Only in Nigeria...

Someone may ask why we are not screaming as before. The simple reason is that as we grow older in age and wiser in wisdom we tend to realize the truth of our predicament. In many societies the trend in change of things moves six steps in the forward direction and two or three steps even four steps backwards. This trend is a natural progression in life. The backward glance sometimes redresses the over active or radical imagination of the citizenry that has pushed a reform that society may not be ready for. In which case the hiccup of change reverses the 'too far' a-leap. In Nigeria, 1960 independence was a step forward, 1963 indigenization policy was ten steps backwards. 1966 coup was two steps backwards. The ensuing war was ten steps backwards, 1970 declaration of no victor no vanquished was five steps forwards. The punishing post war economic policy was one-step backwards. Oil in the delta was two steps forwards, the contracts to mining it was two steps backwards. Refusal to return to civilian rule by Gowon was two steps backwards. Festac was three steps forwards. Coups of the 70's gave a cumulative 4 steps backwards. Shehu Shagari as president was four steps forward. Buhari came in 1993 two steps backwards Babangida two steps backwards, Abacha two steps backwards. Unfair treatment of Abiola' election win eight steps backwards. Shonekan and Abusalami together gave four steps forward. Many serious disturbances of yearly religious crisis in the North and others not counted. Obasanjo gave us six steps forwards. Yaradua two steps forward. Goodluck eight steps forwards. Buhari twenty six steps backwards. We know mathematics: 70 backward steps and 35 forwards steps. Let's use 1960 as our baseline, add 35 to 1960 it gives us 1995, remove 70 from 1995 our answer is 1925. Well now what else do you want me to say. People we are now in 1925 whereas other nations are in the 2000 years or exactly in 2018 as we write. Now tell me what else a sane individual can say to us. I will say it again and again "THE STATE OF A PEOPLE, A NATION, OR RACE IS EXACTLY HOW THEY WANT IT TO BE." Therefore I have whole heartedly rejected our way of life. Let no one tell me of patriotism, of nationalism, of ours and theirs or any such talks. I have rejected us because I cannot be counted as acquiescent to this contraption which we have decided must ever be a roller coaster to hell. Count me out entirely. Maybe in the next 100 years my progeny can make their decision as I have made mine. Life is for the living I would not be part of this death March of Nigeria, I am a Biafran.

Our Homeland is what we make it.

I am very vocal and a fighter indeed. Issues that come at me, get hit with deliberate force, usually it is never the same after I might have run through them. That is the design potential of the machine: me. Now get to the present day and the state of the world as it is. There is a constant gradient that falls and rises from one generation to the other according to the character of both the father and his sons to establish self against the trend of the 'wheels' of natural selection. Nothing with emphasis stands the test of time especially in our society, if it cannot be tried and tested in the fires of that time. The failure to establish and the rise of new guards creates a political tsunami that drags and churns and washes and erodes and decimates and clears the path of the flowing power. But then, I can see the mistakes of yesterday entrenched all over again. The joy of success and the feel of emerging influence. The sound of victory and the cacophony of adulations, but know that the din of the crowd in the brouhaha confuses the wise. It taints the wisdom and redirects our efforts from the primal instincts of our survival. In the end, the cycle moves again a testimony of our poor choices and the failure to maintain a strict principle in our desire to excel. I, the me, as an instrument forged from the fires of a late battle, who have struck gold by dint of hard work and an insatiable desire for excellence is but a single cog in the wheels of destiny. This position when not held with wisdom and a great sense of responsibility have just succeeded in pushing the gradient to the negative by being overtly insensitive to the primary function of my success. My name is not Iwunna. My name is Uwanuruochi. Iwunna the person, the man, the gene, the character, the present and the next shift in the circle of existence is he that stands following my exit. There you can see what this journey really achieved. As for this writer, the perceived present, the obvious present, the man pulled up from the rising hero of yesterday and the force of yesterday's tsunami, he who followed from the additive gradient and multiplied it, he is but the product of yesterday's battle fought and won by another. Who or what I am will only show when the wheel turns over. Therefore never make the same mistake twice... I do not intend to, Biafra is not a choice it is our only home.

Training is more than an exercise, it is everything

In the early days, it was good for me to let it be when things go against me. Really, the church trained me to believe God knows the truth and that is more important. This led to many sad times for me. People grow up believing they can offload their sadness or problems on people like me. Well, in such times, the truth itself suffers.

You read the newspapers, you listen to radio and watch television, may I ask how you feel? As the master of thought, or an opinion leader in your professional field. How do you feel when the governor goes on air to spend thirty minutes lying to himself and to us all? How do you feel when Lai Mohammed drops a few of his comments? When the villagers are put to confusion, looking for where the way out is. Do we not realize Nigeria is entirely without a leader today? Since no one hopes on the words of our, so called leaders. Are you ready to believe there is any program for our progress as a nation in the short or long term?

Their promises are fake, their intentions are different from their spoken words. Their tomorrow does not have you and I written there in. We exist just to be used and discarded. Why then am I calling you to witness this today? Because our common in-action is not propping up this status quo, it is legitimizing it. The common mantra is "if you can't beat them join them." If you ask me, because of our agreement: this is what we want, does mean realizing that I can't beat them, I won't join them? I will not! We: Biafra, will not also accept loads not meant for us. The state of a people, a community, a state, a nation is exactly how they want it. Prove me wrong? Nnamdi Kalu stood and was counted, he made a difference, I hope we can build on his success. You must use your wisdom to change the times. Tomorrow is not ours, unless we beckon on it.

Global village was the catch-word of Marshall McLuhan, which came to reality with Ted Turner when he was building the CNN. It did work as it should, because the military have been using satellite information systems for very many years; spying on each other and selectively picking out THEIR enemies at will. I do not wish to digress here. In a few years, from then, telecommunication satellites filled the skies and countries stumbled over each other to launch theirs or to key into other countries satellites. Tell me how the five super powers made peace, as much as to jointly own the international space center. Tell me how a US astronaut, a Russian cosmonaut, a French space engineer, a British mathematician, a South African tourist, a German surgeon and an Arab billionaire can share living spaces aboard the International Space Center. At what point in this journey of discovery did racism, religion, language, color, and nationality disappear? Yet you want me to believe that we are different. No, what happens is that YOU CREATE THE

ARTIFICIAL BARRIER WHEN IT SUITS YOU. In the mid 90's BBC and CNN and VOA where beaming live all over the world, the Otokoto murder and Owerri peoples' anger in the face of a gang of criminals who kill for the love of money. The 1990s' my friend! Not in the age of wireless systems. We in Nigeria then did not own phones, only those with families abroad called home to ask what was going on in Nigeria. That was how we knew that the world was watching. You can imagine a British presenter trying to pronounce OTOKOTO.

Then, today, in an age when a primary school child will dribble his parents with ICT and networks; when my son in secondary school can write programs for a computer game. When we live-stream a walk in the evening. When I video-call across planet 'earth' like I am eating candy. You mean you want me to assume that Isha Sessay who pulled Nigerian generals apart because of the fake Chibok girls has retired? What of Richard Quest, Amanpour, and all the die-hard 'truth' seekers. Has truth suddenly changed suits? Has the dark continents' fear of malaria taken hold? So now, all at once the media equipment had contrived to break down and the Biafran sufferings are not news worthy. All of a sudden, the people who gave the world Phillip Emeagwali, do not deserve to live in their own homes. The parents, brothers, sisters and relations of Kanu Nwankwo, Okocha, Peter Konyekwachie and others. Millions of doctors and other professionals serving in your countries are Igbo. The silent masters of their work. Well, and the fraudsters too. Your voices are now dead because Igbos have not crossed that threshold that blurs division. We carry no guns, we are not terrorists and life is sacred to us. Let it be. But we, the children of ChukwuOkikeAbiama (God the creator and the originator of all things), know all things. Right or not Igbo deserve a homeland and the answer is not Nigeria. When they wake up tell those news satellite networks that even from the afterlife truth will forever win.

Reference

Barbara Harff and Ted Robert Gurr, (1998) 'The etiology of genocide'; 'Systematic early warning of humanitarian emergencies', Journal of Peace Research, Vol. 35, No. 5, 1998, pp. 551–579.

Made in the USA
Columbia, SC
10 May 2025

57704349R00128